Restorative Justice in Practice

Conflict, connection, and violence

Mayara Carvalho

Translated by Júlia Muinhos

Instituto Pazes

Belo Horizonte, Brazil

2022

Contact info:
E-mail: mdecarvalho@live.com
Instagram: @maylizarb
Academia.edu: https://mayaracarvalho.academia.edu/
Site: www.pazes.com.br

Carvalho, Mayara.
Restorative Justice in Practice: Conflict, connection, and violence / Mayara Carvalho. – Belo Horizonte: Instituto Pazes, 2022.

190 f.

ISBN 9798843027919

1. Law. 2. Restorative Justice. 3. Conflict. 4. Connection. 5. Violence

"[...]
As thought shapes the shaper

Falls heavy on the page, is heard.

All fuses now, falls into place

"[...] From wish to action, word to silence,
My work, my love, my time, my face
Gathered into one intense
Gesture of growing like a plant.
As slowly as the ripening fruit
Fertile, detached, and always spent,
Falls but does not exhaust the root, [...].

May Sarton, Now I become myself.

I'd like to thank Gustavo Silveira Siqueira, my husband, and this book's first reader. How many of my works are not being completed every day in our coexistence, my love?
"Happiness is only real when shared."

Summary

INITIAL CONSIDERATIONS 13

1 RESTORATIVE JUSTICE AND/IN CONNECTION 21

    1.1 Restorative Justice and narrativity 31

    1.2 Complementary considerations about community and connection within Restorative Justice 49

    1.3 The importance of building connection through what it is, and not by shared scarcity 58

2 RESTORATIVE JUSTICE AND/IN CONFLICT 63

    2.1 Micro-community and conflict transformation 75

    2.2 Narrativity and being otherly in conflict 86

    2.3 Security and citizenship: breaking with the single-story in polarized conflicts 96

3 RESTORATIVE JUSTICE AND/IN VIOLENCE 116

    3.1 Accountability in Restorative Justice 127

    3.2 Restorative Justice, violence, and *moral imagination* 136

    3.3 From narratives of violence to community transformation: the case of the Anne Frank Municipal School 144

REFERENCES 173

ABOUT THE AUTHOR: ACADEMIC PATH 186

ABOUT THE AUTHOR: MY WORDS 189

ABOUT THE TRANSLATOR 191

AUTHOR'S NOTE

In another opportunity, I published my Ph.D. thesis almost unchanged in the book "Restorative Community Justice: an experience in Contagem-MG". I had several issues with its contents, but ultimately, I believed that publishing it right away would help at least these two aspects: a) Accepting that a work can always be improved and that even the written word isn't definitive; b) Allowing time and dialogue with other readers to contribute to the book's improvement.

In that sense, I thought I would publish a second edition with updates, revisions, and additions that would reflect the wealth of this contact with different perspectives.

However, something about this idea still didn't sit right with me. That book has about 400 pages, a lot of them portraying my research methodology or bringing a very academic perspective to the text.

I believed that could drive away or at least tire those who practice and study Restorative Justice but aren't exactly researchers themselves. At the same time, I thought that the wealth brought by field research held a lot of value even for these people. So, suddenly, I caught myself reflecting on the real use of putting another purely theoretical book on Restorative Justice into the world.

That was when I opted for another path: I decided to publish this book, which is focused on the praxis of Restorative Justice according to the tripod Conflict, Connection, and Violence. A lot of it is entirely new, and other parts are the revision and updates of some of the text from my Ph.D. thesis.

This way, I try to unite the accessibility of content with the wealth of primary data collected through years of empirical research.

And, just like my last book, this "work is completed in the other". It makes more sense now that it has come to you.

Belo Horizonte-Brazil, April 2021.

INITIAL CONSIDERATIONS

More and more each day, I realize the importance of being intentional about the theories that underlie our practices. And if that's important in a general sense when one works with conflict and connection, it's even more so when you're dealing with a vision of justice that can be put into practice through several methods - or even none at all.

My research and practices in Restorative Justice have shown me that it is essential to be intentional about questions such as "what will happen if we choose this one process, and not another?", "which actors should be involved?", "what do these people believe in?", "which dialogues need to take place?", "what are the goals of each party?", "what can be done to help these people achieve their goals?".

Without this sort of intentionality, I believe a lot of our time would be spent looking for answers to questions we don't truly understand and – because we don't, would be hard to find.

More than searching for answers, we need to truly examine and dwell on these questions.

Rene Descartes used to say that we don't describe the world that we see; on the contrary, we only see the world that we're capable of describing. Since one of the principles of Restorative Justice is the transformation of conflicts, communities, and relationships, the exercise to "change lenses" – developed by Howard Zehr – demands intentionality about the theories that underlie our practices.

This book's goal is to start a conversation about some reflections I've been developing for the last few years of research and facilitation of restorative practices. It is not a doctrine of irrefutable truths. Rather, it is a step in the effort for the collective construction of conscience and intentionality in the Restorative Justice that we are building and improving in Brazil.

And although I am its only author, this book as it exists today is the result of what I was able to learn due to my contact with other facilitators and parties in restorative practices; and with the subjects and communities who participated in my research.

Before I continue, I think it's important to emphasize that, specifically regarding the empirical data resulting from my Ph.D. research, the narratives and elements that I will present throughout this book were the result of interviews with local leaders, users, and implementers of the

"Security with Citizenship Joint Program: preventing violence and strengthening citizenship with a focus on children, teenagers and young people in vulnerable conditions in Brazilian communities" – in the administrative region of Nacional, in the city of Contagem, state of Minas Gerais.

As I highlighted in the presentation,[1] I talk more about the methodology and data from this research in another work. Here, I will only present what I consider fundamental to provide a good comprehension of this intentionality regarding the theories that guide our practices. I will do that supported by the tripod "Connection, Conflict and Violence", which I believe builds the foundations for the Restorative Justice practices.

Still in these introductory lines, I will briefly introduce the researched Program, so that the reader may have a contextual notion of the

---

[1] Cf. Carvalho, Mayara. (2019). *Justiça Restaurativa na Comunidade: uma experiência em Contagem-MG.*

situation and background that I am talking about when presenting the data.

Security with Citizenship came to life from the collective efforts of different United Nations (UN) agencies, in partnership with Brazilian communities and municipal public administration. Having practices centered around violence prevention and building and strengthening citizenship as its goals, the Program was focused on children, teenagers, and young people in situations of vulnerability.

In Brazil, the *Security with Citizenship Program* went from 2010 to 2013, covering the municipalities of Contagem, in Minas Gerais, Lauro de Freitas, in Bahia, and Vitória, in Espírito Santo. My research, though, was limited to the analysis of effectiveness in Contagem, especially in the Nacional - the peripheral administrative region in which the Program's actions were centered.

According to the accounts and interviews from my field research, the greatest highlight of *Security with Citizenship* was its utilization of the United Nations Development Programme's (UNDP) methodology, which considered the local resources and potentialities and included community agents in each step of the decision-making and execution of projects, programs, services, and public policies

The Program's practices were developed to build and strengthen: the bonds of belonging and meaning within the region; the community's participation and influence in public administration and decision-making instances related to matters that affected it; the active and expanded accountability of residents, centering their own identification of their needs and the impacts of their actions; the understanding of the damage caused and revealed by harmful acts as a way to prevent violence; and social transformation.

In this book, I will share several narratives to demonstrate part of these practices and their impacts.

As I've done in other works, I point out that I've chosen to use singular they/them pronouns throughout this book, to best include all readers and decenter the notions of neutrality from the masculine pronouns.

1 RESTORATIVE JUSTICE AND/IN CONNECTION

Four of the most spread-out myths related to Restorative Justice (RJ) are a product of the confusion between it and a) adequate methods for dealing with conflicts; b) circular practices; c) mediation; d) a practice preferably applied in the criminal system.

In the end, these four misconceptions come from ignoring the same basilar truth: the fact that restorative practices are aimed, more than anything, to build and strengthen connection.

It's not without reason that this book starts with the most fundamental (and the most forgotten) basis of the RJ tripod. That way, even if the reader gives up in the book's first pages, they will still have had contact with its most essential notion.

Restorative Justice proposes a different vision of justice, with new lenses through which we see conflicts, violence, and connections. That doesn't mean it doesn't entail adequate methods to deal with conflicts. It does, to the extent that Restorative Justice can be put into practice through various methods, including circular processes. It is important to stress, though, that the restorative practice isn't composed only of these methods.

Thereby, I want to highlight that, even though it is common to use certain methods and preconceived techniques to materialize our practices, the *restorative continuum* comports approaches, practices, and processes that go beyond these methods.

For a practice to be considered restorative, what matters is its contents, not necessarily its form. That is, what guarantees that it a practice is indeed restorative is if it respects

RJ's principles, fundamentals, and values. In other words: the practice must be, essentially, the materialization of RJ's vision of justice.

In addition to that, it must be said that it is incompatible with Restorative Justice's ancestral origins to intend for its experiences to presuppose an association with conflict and violence.

The meaning of RJ's practices was built through work with the connection between human groups, which does include situations of conflict and violence but isn't limited to them.

It is possible — and desired — that restorative practices are used even before there's is any violence or incompatibility of goals. We can make use of the restorative vision of justice as a way to: deepen relationships that are already going well at the moment; bring people that already live in harmony together; reinforce bonds of belonging and meaning in work environments; build schools as spaces of socioemotional safety and support; enable families and communities to know each better and get closer; among many other possibilities.

If we solidify Restorative Justice's foundations in connection and practice it with that in mind, we are very likely to have less violence and more acceptance in our social bonds.

To believe that Restorative Justice can only be practiced when there is conflict or violence is to reduce it to a lot less than it can be. The greatest transformative potential of RJ is precisely in its practices focused on connection.

This is because RJ's vision of justice seeks to satisfy basic human needs, and few things bring as much satisfaction as the intentional creation of safe spaces aimed at building and deepening connections with belonging and meaning.

With all that said, I imagine you already understood that RJ's great place of practice is not exactly in the criminal area. Still, this misconception is very common in Brazil. I believe that it stems from two factors: a) the fact that RJ's dissemination in Brazil was largely promoted by the Judiciary, with practices developed mainly within criminal cases; b) the importance and propagation of Professor Howard Zehr's[2] work in the country, given that most of his RJ practices are applied precisely in crime-related cases.

Now that I've addressed this common misconception, I'd like to highlight some of the restorative vision of justice's essential elements.

The restorative vision of justice aims to intentionally build safe and cooperative spaces, based primarily in narrativity and personal storytelling, to a) develop and deepen connection with belonging and meaning; b) satisfy the participants' basic human needs; c) when it is the case, repair damages and heal individual and

---

[2] Zehr, Howard. (2015). *Changing lenses: restorative justice for our times*. (Twenty-fifth-anniversary edition). Herald Press.

collective traumas; d) solve and transform conflicts, relationships and communities e) deal with the impacts, whether intentional or not, of the participants' actions in situations of interdependence; f) when fitting, ensure the construction of a safe space in which it is possible to identify the impacts of the participant's actions, as well as pre-existing dynamics that were revealed by those actions; g) when appropriate, provide adequate information that enables active responsibility of the participants themselves in regards to the consequences of their acts; h) when applicable, ensure participation and provide adequate information so that people indirectly implicated by the facts dealt with in RJ's practices can assume their share of responsibility or protagonism regarding the conditions and context in which those facts took place; i) prevent and end violence, whether individual or collective, physical or psychological, verbal or non-verbal, exceptional or structural, motivated or unmotivated.

From what has been said so far, note that conflict and violence may be what move Restorative Justice practice, but they aren't necessary for it. Regardless, one thing is certain: RJ will be connection-oriented.

This connection won't be necessarily built between the central participants in a conflict, but there will always be a focus on the construction of belonging and meaning of each participant within their referral and support micro-community.

For you to understand this point better, I need to talk a little about the concept of community in RJ. Within this vision of justice, "community" is defined as a human grouping based on links of belonging and meaning.

Even with the knowledge about its past and its future possibilities, the Restorative Justice community is defined in the present, being a product of the continuous and provisory dialogues established between its members.

This occurs because the community isn't defined aprioristically, with the inflexibility of an *imagined community*[3], it is – instead – a process and, as such, an open creation. Likewise, the community members are not its starting point, but its becoming. With good reason, Alfonso Torres Carrillo[4] highlights that

> **Community is not a subjectivity created from the sum of previously constituted individual subjectivities, but an inter-subjectivity generated from *being-with* others.**
> In a community, every one of its members is *alter*, the "other" who surprises, seduces, or lacerates us, but with which we irrevocably cohabit; they are

---

[3] Cf. Anderson, Benedict. (1993). *Comunidades imaginadas: reflexiones sobre el origen y la difusión del nacionalismo.* Cultura Libre.
[4] Carrillo, Alfonso Torres. (2017). *El retorno a la comunidad: problemas, debates y desafíos de vivir juntos.* Fundación Centro Internacional de Educación y Desarrollo Humano. pp. 213-214.

difference and otherness[5]: **the person from the community doesn't exist by "themself", they are necessarily "another",** a chain of change that never fully locks into a new identity. **The community assumes an irreducible heterogeneity of the subjects that conform it and conform to it**. *[free translation[6]] [emphasis added]*

---

[5] The original term used here was *otredad*, translated into "otherness" in an attempt to communicate the ideas of alterity and opposition simultaneously understood in the Spanish term. The same occurs when I use the adverb *otherly* in other moments of this book. With *otherness*, I intend to refer to the complex concept of the other as the one we never were, are or will be, and also the one we don't want to be. In this sense, even when arranged in the singular, the other is multiple: as many as I am not. The singular here lies in that I am not the other. Not only that, but the content of the other is also variable according to the different perspectives: in the same way that someone is my other, I am someone's other. The concept is, therefore, relational and variable.

[6] In the original: "La comunidad no es una subjetividad resultada de la suma de unas subjetividades individuales previamente constituidas, sino una intersubjetividad que se gesta a partir del ser-con otros.

En una comunidad, cada integrante es alter, es el otro, que nos sorprende, seduce o lacera, pero con el cual, cohabitamos irrevocablemente; es diferencia y otredad: el sujeto de la comunidad no es el 'sí mismo, sino necesariamente un 'otro', una cadena de alteraciones que nunca se fija en una nueva identidad. La comunidad supone una heterogeneidad irreductible de los sujetos que la conforman y que se conforman en ella".

From this perspective, the community narrative must contemplate its diversity, constantly reassessing whether the dominant stories have been corresponding to those desired by its members.

Restorative Justice aims to reach a state of peace with voice, of participative peace.

Having made these considerations about the concept of community itself, I would like to emphasize that, within restorative practices, participants do not usually coincide with the central poles of a conflict, even when one does exist.

In traditional law, for example, we usually have two opposite poles - the plaintiff and the defendant, or even the victim and the offender. Restorative Justice, however – through considering the gregarious component of the human condition – understands that people indirectly involved in a situation can be essential to achieve its transformation.

This participation doesn't happen by chance, nor is it presupposed. It is, in fact, the directly involved people who name and specify other actors they would like to be present in the practice.

Their presence usually takes place so that a) the practices are more comfortable; b) immediately involved participants feel supported; c) there can be a deeper understanding of the case's impacts, talents, resources, and potentials; d) bonds are deepened and belonging is built.

1.1 Restorative Justice and narrativity

Restorative Justice recognizes that being conscious and able to appropriate your own personal stories are, on their own, elements that potentialize connection and restoration (understood as the recovery of a better past or as the construction of a new beginning).

For that reason, the restorative practice starts with questions – as an invite for the person to place themselves and see their position within their own story.

One of the most important abilities of the RJ facilitator is precisely their tools and techniques to bring up the fundamental questions to propel significant reflections to the issue at hand – be they subjective or collective.

A question is always an invitation: an invite to presence, an invitation to reflection. Besides that, it is also an invitation to take protagonism, since the answer must be offered through the "I" pronoun, the first person singular. That is, evasive speech patterns that refer generically "to the system", "the people", and "humanity" should be avoided.

In this sense, neither should one speak as if they occupied the other's place. Each person speaks about themselves, from their point of view, about their feelings and their needs. And each person is given the opportunity, if they want, to hear what the others narrate about themselves.

Regarding this aspect, it is important to emphasize that a very common way for violence to be manifested is through the illegitimate exercise of power when one tells the story of another person or collective – and then proceeds to make this outside perspective the definitive version of that individual or group's story[7]. When this is done with the support of the State, the single-story takes on the contour of officialdom and can be even more damaging to the community at hand.

If what's been seized is connected to the part of the narrative in which the focus is at the

---

[7] Adichie, Chimamanda Ngozi. (2009, October 7th). *The danger of the single story*. YouTube. https://www.youtube.com/watch?v=D9Ihs241zeg.

moment, everyone must see themselves as capable of telling their own stories.

When focusing on violence, impotence, or the absence of a group of people, for example, the perspective established will probably teach through the production of trauma. Repetition gives the single-story an air of normalcy, which is then confused with the real recollection of the events.

In that sense, the problem of the single story isn't that it is false, it can often be true; the problem is its incompleteness – the fact that it doesn't consider the diversity and complexity of the situation at hand[8].

When only one version of the narrative is presented, a reduced and limiting understanding of the matters inherent to it is formed. This is determinant, since the way one perceives a

---

[8] Olb Jon; Parry, Madeleine. (2018). *Hannah Gadsby: Nanette* [Live Comedy Performance]. Netflix.

situation directly affects what one can think of as its possible causes and solutions [9].

Another sensitive point in terms of violence when telling another person or group's story is to start it from the second thing that happened. That is, selecting the aspects of it one believes to be worth consideration and ignoring others. Here, once again, the knowledge that a story is determined by the perspective from which it is told is important[10].

To give an example, I'll tell a story I've come in contact with during my Ph.D. research.

In one of the Nacional neighborhoods, Confisco, this harmful practice was especially present: the neighborhood was defined and depictured mainly for the lack of rights and services in its population lives, with a direct

---

[9] Zehr, Howard. (2015). *Changing lenses: restorative justice for our times*. (Twenty-fifth-anniversary edition). Herald Press.
[10] Adichie, Chimamanda Ngozi. (2009, October 7th). *The danger of the single story*. YouTube. https://www.youtube.com/watch?v=D9Ihs241zeg.

reflection on the presence of violence there. The neighborhood is located between the cities of Contagem and Belo Horizonte and suffers routinely from allegations from both municipalities' administrators that the neighborhood isn't their responsibility, but the other's.

Created three decades ago as a consequence of a squatting promoted by 160 homeless families, Confisco was built without State support or access to resources: its first homes were made of canvas, without water supply, electricity, sewage, transportation, or paving. Since the neighborhood wasn't included in the garbage collection services and had a hilly, rough terrain, one of its lowest areas – the "big hole" was turned into a waste disposal location, which led to the presence of rats, cockroaches, snakes, scorpions, and insects in the community[11].

---

[11] Data provided by the residents and by the Centro de Referência Popular do Bairro do Confisco (People's

Even though since then there has been a considerable betterment of the living conditions in Confisco, which nowadays has treated water, a sewerage system, electricity, and pavement on the streets, the fact that it occupies two municipalities still brings many hardships to its residents' daily lives. In that context, the ones who suffer the most seem to be those who live in the part of the neighborhood located in Contagem, since they don't have access to the Basic Health Unit located nearby and live in the territory's most socially vulnerable place.

In lieu of this reality, the community has articulated solidarity networks that go from the offering of support when some families were made homeless by landslides, to the *WhatsApp*

Reference Center of the Confisco Neighborhood). As for the latter, similar accounts can be accessed on the center's Facebook page. Cf.: Centro de Referência Popular do Bairro do Confisco. (2014, March 21) *Histórico do Conjunto Confisco*. Facebook. https://www.facebook.com/confiscobh/posts/hist%C3%B3ric o-do-conjunto-confiscoo-conjunto-confisco-nasceu-em-1988- e-est%C3%A1-localiza/440726819404942/.

groups initiative's "Confisco pela Paz" (in Portuguese, "Confisco for Peace"). Even so, the low self-esteem that guided the community's perspective of itself was still very present, based on the perpetuation of the single-story which defined Confisco by its needs and the presence of violence in the territory.

The neighborhood's name itself carried a stigma and wasn't liked by its oldest residents, who had even tried to change it to honor a community leader instead. They weren't successful, though, and the name Confisco remained.

One of the community's oldest leaders, Maria das Graças Silva Ferreira – known as Graça –, had recognized the need to tell the neighborhood's story from the perspective of its successful fight for housing instead of focusing on its marginalized condition. Graça wanted to create a document, which she thought could be a comic book, to distribute to the residents and consolidate this alternative narrative about the community[12].

To her, the comic book format was important because it would grant an interest in the contents of the document and its subsequent circulation among residents. Even though her dream was long-lived, Graça did not see any possibilities to materialize it. Still, she constantly brought it up to other community leaders. The opportunity, however, came with the involvement of the Municipal School Anne Frank (Escola

---

[12] Information obtained from interviews with Sandra Mara and Moacir Fagundes Freitas, as well as conversations with Graça, children who study at Anne Frank Municipal School and other residents of Confisco. There is also reference to this story in the series "Confisco: História Revista", which generated three news articles produced by Jornal Minas, from Rede Minas. Cf. Rede Minas. Jornal Minas. (2018). *Série Confisco: História Revista – Episódio 1.* Youtube. https://www.youtube.com/watch?v=wM86YIgFe-A.; Rede Minas. Jornal Minas. (2018). *Série Confisco: História Revista – Episódio 2.* YouTube. https://www.youtube.com/watch?v=75z_K7DtFAI&feature=youtu.be.; Rede Minas. Jornal Minas. *Série Confisco: História Revista – Episódio 3.* (2018). YouTube. https://www.youtube.com/watch?v=73fTyKoB5Xc..

Municipal Anne Frank - EMAF) with the idea, from the initiative of the History Teacher, Moacir Fagundes Freitas, and the then Principal, Sandra Mara Vicente – a friend of Graça who put the teacher and the community leader in contact.

The teacher had noticed that the students were ashamed to identify themselves as residents of the neighborhood, preferring to make indirect references to the locality – usually talking about its proximity to the Zoo gate instead of mentioning Confisco. Moacir narrates:

> It all started because I noticed how frequent little conflicts in the classroom were, and that the source of these conflicts was that the majority of the boys and girls were ashamed to say they belonged to Confisco. When those little classroom fights happened, they would say "ah, but I don't live here. You're from Confisco, right?. You are a 'confisquer', I'm not". **No one ever lived at Confisco, everyone said they lived in nearby neighborhoods.** [...] Nobody

admitted it. **The majority of them were ashamed of saying they were from Confisco. It was a way of mocking – calling the other a "confisquer". I noticed that and realized I couldn't teach European History when an issue like that was hitting me in the face at all times there. That started to bother me and I began to ask them: "hey, you all, why do you think living here is so bad? Does anyone know the history of this neighborhood? Does anyone know why it has this name?".** And then someone said, "uh, teacher, I know one thing. I know it was a farm". When I threw these questions back at them, they started to feel motivated. "let's research it, then! Are you all in? If no one wants to live here at Confisco, let's try to get to know the neighborhood first, to know if that's really true". Then, I scheduled a class in the bleachers with them. In that class, I took a scale model of the neighborhood that the school had before this project. [...] Some history interns were arriving [at the school] and that was one of the first classes I had with them. I knew that a community leader would go to the school that day, she was one of the founders [of the neighborhood]. Besides her, an employee who was also one of our founders was there too. **They loved to see the scale model and started pointing out where their homes were.** And then, I asked the reason why the neighborhood's name was Confisco, about how it had started. **When I threw all these questions they couldn't answer at them, I told them there was a way to find those answers – that, at that moment, we had in the school a community leader and an employee that had participated in the neighborhood's founding, and I asked them to look for that information.** They left the bleachers and went running to the two women. [...] The two started talking and the girls and boys got super excited to be listening to things about the neighborhood's origins in the voice of these people. *[emphasis added]*

After identifying the rejection of belonging and identity with the territory, Moacir tried to work on this issue-problem in the classroom with the school's 7th-grade students, in 2016. In the subsequent classes, he started questioning them about the neighborhood's image. It was then he asked why the students had so strongly denied belonging there, and if they had ever perceived this behavior in other residents too.

These questions encouraged the students to get interested in becoming involved in a research project aiming to identify what image the residents had of the neighborhood. A questionnaire was formulated with questions that ranged from the residents' impression of Confisco, passing through their living conditions, to a question on if they had ever needed to hide that they lived there. In some of the questions, the image that other people had of the neighborhood was also addressed.

The teacher made badges for the students which identified them as "historians" or "researchers". He distributed clipboards to each of them and formed smaller groups that followed him and the new interns around the community. He reports that the students were proud and excited from the very beginning, commenting on the fact that they were now researchers and historians.

As he tells, the data tabulation was done on the day following their gathering. Both the questions in the questionnaires and the data tabulation were built with the students, ensuring that they participated in the entire research process.

The teacher also went with his interns to the Minas Gerais' Public Archive (Arquivo Público Mineiro) and the Belo Horizonte's Public Archive (Arquivo Público de Belo Horizonte). There they collected old photos of the neighborhood, and then showed copies of them to the students. The photos were accompanied by old and current newspaper headlines covering the neighborhood. In this first research effort, the professor and the interns only identified negative headlines, most referring to murder, robbery, and trafficking.

According to Moacir,

> When we showed the old and new headlines to the students with *PowerPoint*... You should have seen what happened in the classroom! **I call this class "the indignation class". The students were outraged by the headlines, it was a riot. There was an uproar. I remember this little girl saying: "we'll call this reporter here for him to say what he wrote about our neighborhood to our faces. Our neighborhood is nothing like this". I decided to channel this indignation into learning.** I asked how we could show this guy that Confisco isn't only what the headlines show. **Then, the intern, Luiza, gave us the idea of taking pictures of the neighborhood, since we could communicate that through photos.** [...] Luiza and two other interns offered, then, a

workshop on photography techniques. *[added emphasis]*.

Regarding the "indignation class", it is important to keep in mind that

> [...] when we look at a subaltern community of gender, ethnicity, class, or sexual orientation in the countryside or the city, we do not see the particularities of each of them: the patronized social imaginary identifies exactly that – a pattern that, as a homogenizing category, only allows us to encode the stereotype with which we were taught to communicate. And the stereotype only exists within solid and clearly established borders[13].

Moacir believes that the history he teaches shouldn't be abstract, without any connection to the students' day-to-day. He always

---

[13] Amaral Filho, Nemézio C. (2008). As perigosas fronteiras da "comunidade": um desafio à comunicação comunitária. In.: Paiva, Raquel; Santos, Cristiano Henrique Ribeiro dos. (Eds.). *Comunidade e contra-hegemonia: rotas de comunicação alternativa.* (p. 81). Mauad X: FAPERJ.

sought to connect the history class's context with the neighborhood's reality. Therefore, when he realized that the students had incorporated the single, "official" narrative about Confisco in their lives and that they were reproducing this understanding of the neighborhood, he dedicated himself to restoring the history of the territory – with a focus on citizenship, belonging and meaning.

Since the Municipal School Anne Frank was the first building in the neighborhood, both the principal and the teacher understood that the school was a qualified space for this restoration, considering that it had an important social function to that community.

This is confirmed in Graça's account depicted in the comic, according to which the school is the heart of the neighborhood. This imagery is also highlighted by Ms. Fátima – whose account is also present in the comic – who said that Anne Frank Municipal School "isn't a school, it is a community... it's everything together, I think. Because the school, we see it as a... it's a place we know we can count on.

This perception isn't exclusive to these two leaders. A transformative school, the Anne Frank Municipal School is closely connected to Confisco's community in a way that crosses the physical limits of its walls – which seem to delimit where the school begins and where the street ends.

Various projects are routinely conducted to guarantee that, ranging from the opening of the School's space so the community members can use its football field; to holding festivities, school activities, and events in the neighborhood's squares and streets, inviting residents to take part in them.

This type of attitude, according to Sandra Mara, was essential to reduce student dropout rates and violence at the school, preserve the students' lives, and strengthen the connection between the school community and other Confisco residents. Before these initiatives, the presence of armed students and harassment of students by adults from the community linked to crime, among other frequent violent occurrences were common at the School[14]. Instead of waiting for a scenario favorable for transformation, it was the School's proposal of alterity and acceptance that transformed its environment.

The comic book made by the students under the coordination of teacher Moacir Fagundes will be addressed in detail on the topic "Restorative Justice and/in violence".

---

[14] Data supported by internal school documents to which I had access during my field research.

1.2 Complementary considerations about community and connection within Restorative Justice

The local is the main space of the community. But what are we talking about when we talk about community? Being it a recurrent term in everyday language in Brazil, there are two meanings commonly attributed to the term: one refers to geographical spaces marked by economic poverty and the violation or threat of violation of fundamental rights; and the other is focused on belonging to specific groups, like the "LGBTQ community", a "religious community", a "school community" or even an "academic community". In both these meanings, the term seems to lack density[15].

---

[15] Carrillo, Alfonso Torres. (2017). *El retorno a la comunidad: problemas, debates y desafíos de vivir juntos.* Fundación Centro Internacional de Educación y Desarrollo Humano. p. 11.

Sometimes, "community" is defined in a residual way: community is what we don't *yet* have and what we aim to achieve There's also an undefined idea of community that links it to ancestry and wisdom. In this case, the term is usually evoked by native peoples, remnant populations of quilombos, or even by rural, urban, or black social movements. It so happens that, in these situations, the term is often used defensively, in contrast to the outsider, hegemonic "other" way of being, conceived as "anti-community"[16].

In this case, it symbolizes the rescue of a lost community or, at least, an invisible one in the abstract imaginary of the individual. This understanding, however, often arrives at a place of self-limitation, with the confusion of ancestry and a single, very specific way of constituting

---

[16] Carrillo, Alfonso Torres. (2017). *El retorno a la comunidad: problemas, debates y desafíos de vivir juntos.* Fundación Centro Internacional de Educación y Desarrollo Humano. pp. 13, 197.

oneself within this collective. This happens when there's an attachment to a – more or less idealized – past, when this identity group lived in peace and harmony.

The community to which restorative justice refers, though linked to ancestry, is not nostalgic: it is an emancipatory, political, and ethical option,[17] always constituted in the present,

> [...] the true evil present in today's political life, consists [...] of the fact the man sees his fellow man as something he can experience, discover, that is, that he can enjoy in his usefulness, in his applicability. [...] That's what must be surpassed. There is, however, a big obstacle in the way, and that is the false radicalism of today's youth. This youth satisfies itself by representing things as follows: there is an ideal form of being to things, for example, an ideal State or society. It can be only

---

[17] Carrillo, Alfonso Torres. (2017). *El retorno a la comunidad: problemas, debates y desafíos de vivir juntos.* Fundación Centro Internacional de Educación y Desarrollo Humano. p. 217.

reached, in a way... in a certain political or revolutionary way, and therefore it cannot be reached in the here and now. With this delay, the basis for a life without fulfillment is established. Therefore, here and now, one participates only in what is valid at this moment. This is radicalism as escapism. [...]

On the opposite side of that, **one recognizes the dividing line that is drawn each and every day. Today, this is what can be done by me, among us, in this life that is given to us; and that's what cannot be done. [...] That is what responsibility means. And if we take this concept in its whole, responsibility always means responsibility towards someone.** Responsibility towards oneself is an illusion.

True responsibility is always responsibility towards the other. [...] The *hic et nunc*, the here and now responsibility. This is the ultimate point that we, in fact, can reach. Everything else is personal, everything else each man must individually decide for himself and it is a matter of time, depending on his situation, his talent, his possibilities, his location, his moment[18]. *[emphasis added]*

As a process, the community is something perpetually in creation. For the same reason, community members are not a starting point – there is no aprioristic list of included and excluded people–, only the community's becoming. To paraphrase Marshall Sahlins, "the flux is of such a nature that you can never immerse yourself twice in the same community[19]".

As identified in the alternative narrative of Confisco's history developed by the community, its members drove away from the stereotype associated with the community, since it only isolated the other and distanced people as it subjugated them inside the symbolic sphere and imposed a definition of its members from the outside in[20]. A stereotype can only fit within solid

---

[18] BUBER, Martin. (2012). *Sobre comunidade.* Perspectiva. p. 78-79.
[19] Sahlins, Marshall. (2013). Heráclito x Heródoto. In: _____ *Esperando Foucault, ainda.* Cosac Naif, 2013. p. 16.
[20] Bhabha, Homi K. (2003). *O local da cultura.* Editora UFMG.

borders. In the opposite direction, the community – as a process – is forever under construction, being constituted by movement and its always changing borders[21].

In that sense, "the new community's goal is the community itself[22]".

> It [our community] doesn't want to reform; its concern is to transform. [...] In this way, our community does not *want* revolution, it *is* revolution. [...] For us, revolution does not mean destroying old things but living new things. We are not eager to destroy, but eager to create. Our revolution entails the creation of a new life in small circles and pure communities. [...] In this new life, men who due to the specialization of contemporary society have become bodies with a strictly

---

[21] Amaral Filho, Nemézio C. (2008). As perigosas fronteiras da "comunidade": um desafio à comunicação comunitária. In.: Paiva, Raquel; Santos, Cristiano Henrique Ribeiro dos. (Eds). *Comunidade e contra-hegemonia: rotas de comunicação alternativa.* (pp. 75-87). Mauad X: FAPERJ.
[22] Buber, Martin. (2012). *Sobre comunidade.* Perspectiva. p. 33.

well-defined function and who, in order to live, must conform to this function, will once again be capable of drawing from the plenitude. These men will no longer make connections with each other as before, just because specialized men mutually depend on one another – they will meet each other because of love, because of their longing for community, and because of lavish virtue.

Men who in today's society have been thrown into a gear driven by profit in order to atrophy their free creativity under the yoke of profit-seeking work will, in this new life, be elevated to the new order of things, where not the utilitarian principle, but the creative and freer principle of its subdued forces reigns. In this new life, not only the pluricommunity will be reborn in an even newer, more noble, and pure form, but also, and through it, and in it, the bicommunity will be so; and the solitude of the calmest hours of contemplation and creation will uncover a new and richer color. **Each one will live at the same time, inside himself and inside all**[23]. *[emphasis added]*

---

[23] Buber, Martin. (2012). *Sobre comunidade*. Perspectiva. pp.

When considering another person as the living being I'm here for, just as they're here for me, I'm in community[24].

38-39.
[24] Buber, Martin. (2012). *Sobre comunidade.* Perspectiva. p. 88.

1.3 The importance of building connection through what it is, and not by shared scarcity

It is quite common for collectives to be established due to shared challenges their members seek to transform.

This type of connection, albeit strategic, if not centered on the precise identification of what this collective truly is – its resources, talents, and potentialities – may perform below its potential for community transformation.

It is important to emphasize that defining ourselves as "anti" or "against" something does not give us a dimension of what we truly are and how we should act. This type of identification only alerts us to what we are not (or do not wish to be) – which is of little effectiveness.

Beyond the conscience of what we are not, we need to understand our purpose: where we want to go; what does that say about who we are; what are our characteristics, who composes our support network, and what knowledge may help us in our trajectory.

If the main objective of Restorative Justice involves the building of a new beginning, the satisfaction of needs, and transformation, then communities defined as "anti" something are not enough.

To illustrate, I will present the example of the Trilhas da Paz (Trails of Peace, in English) project, which I encountered during the field research for my Ph.D.

Trilhas da Paz aimed to bring attention to educational public spaces such as schools and squares, either to build a positive image of what the territory had already achieved; or to inform the population about the presence of goods and services at their disposal.

This way, whenever they went outside, the residents could easily visualize the resources and potentialities they had around them. The initiative also contributed to making the environment more colorful, and less identified with the characteristic neglect of spaces surrounded by dirt and crime.

Another important aspect is that the signage of these services ended up bringing awareness to many residents who previously didn't know of the existence of some of the resources.

The project understood the collective effort to improve the community space and signal existing goods and services as a political act.

At once, Trilhas da Paz improved the environmental perception of public spaces in the Nacional and enabled teenagers to work with stencils and develop their artistic skills.

Many of the boys who participated in the project were socio-economically vulnerable, with the frequent presence of narratives that entailed constant threats to their lives, or direct involvement with criminal acts or with adults who were known to commit crimes, especially drug trafficking.

In a conversation with the researcher, some of these teens reported that their involvement with urban art distanced them from a destiny that seemed unavoidable: that of living off drug sales or dying because of it.

Beyond that, as Paulo Terrinha highlights:

> I see change, transformation, and freedom [with the *graffiti*] because it includes, perhaps, a boy who would have no prospects of life... even though art in Brazil is not taken seriously, you know? [...] **the mere involvement of a child with art may not make them rich, but the way they see things changes, and this will bring positive consequences later on.** It's the simple things... my gaze changes, the way I see life, how I see the other, how I see the world. So, this will transform who I am and who I will be. This

will directly impact my choices.
[emphasis added]

2 RESTORATIVE JUSTICE AND/IN CONFLICT

Conflict is perhaps the most *mainstream* scope associated with Restorative Justice practice. But, even here, there are several fundamental doubts about the extent and scope of restorative practice.

The most frequent examples of myths related to the field are that RJ can be used to prevent conflicts; that there need to be collective meetings between participants of its practices; that RJ practice is exclusive to the criminal field; and the general vagueness about in which conflicts can RJ be used.

Before more closely approaching the main theme of this chapter, I would like to clarify the understanding of conflict I hold as a premise for working with Restorative Justice.

Initially, I would like to emphasize that I make use here of social interaction theories[25], which understand that only exists conflict because there is interdependence. Even the internal conflicts or those strongly related to structural issues exist because of the gregarious, relational aspect of humanity.

It doesn't matter if, "deep, deep, deep down, we would like our problems to be solved by decree[26]", conflict is a natural and unavoidable element of human coexistence.

---

[25] Cf. Deutsch, Morton. (1986). Cooperation, Conflict, and Justice. In.: Bierhoff, Hans Wermer; Cohen, Ronald; Greenberg, Jerald. (Eds.). *Justice in Social Relations*. Melvin J. Lerner; Deutsch, Morton. (2014). Cooperation, Competition, and Conflict. In.: Coleman, Peter; Deutsch, Morton; Marcus, Eric. (Eds.). *The handbook of conflict resolution: theory and practice*. Jossey-Bass; Calvo Soler, Raúl. (2014). *Mapeo de conflictos: técnica para la exploración de los conflictos*. Gedisa.

[26] Leminski, Paulo. (2013). *Toda Poesia*. Companhia das Letras.

Defined as the incompatibility of goals in a social relationship of interdependence, conflicts can be real or perceived[27]. For this reason, a conflict can exist in a given situation even if everyone involved has the same needs and interests.

Though the unavoidability of conflict in social relations may appear to be something negative or deterministic, it is a fundamental element of transformation, be it at the individual, relational, community, regional, social or international level.

Since there is conflict only in social relations in which there is some sort of interdependence, the subjects involved are co-responsible for its causes, but they also have the autonomy necessary for the participatory construction of transformation.

---

[27] Calvo Soler, Raúl. (2014). *Mapeo de conflictos: técnica para la exploración de los conflictos*. Gedisa,

Therefore, if we're part of a community that tolerates violence and has recurrent conflicts, we must ask ourselves which of our habitual behaviors have allowed or sustained this situation.

Here, a distinction is important: although common sense says otherwise, conflict has no necessary correlation with violence. On the contrary, when we handle conflicts properly, it is unlikely that violence will surface.

The opposite is also true: if we are silent, and do not see or pretend that a conflict is not there, some of the people involved may use violent strategies precisely to force their conflicts to be seen or heard.

In other words: outbursts of violence are usually associated with attempts to be cordial, with a constant avoidance of talking about the "elephant in the room".

However, I'm not advocating that anyone speaks carelessly. That wouldn't even be compatible with Restorative Justice. What I am saying – and I want to be very emphatic in it – is that: you should not seek to prevent conflicts unless you want an explosion of violence!

Conflicts should not be prevented! They should be heard, seen, and taken care of! Restorative Justice can never be used to prevent conflicts. What it intentionally seeks to prevent and put an end to is violence. And, as I said, it is by taking care of conflicts that we prevent violence!

Conflicts are a natural component of social interaction with diversity, they are synonymous with the legitimacy of plural forms of life.

In addition, the existence of conflicts ignites the creative and curious gaze, birthed by the realization that it is possible to live and be happy in many different ways on this Earth.

Precisely for this reason, conflicts are strategic for social transformation. If conflicts didn't exist, I could not even be writing this book and signing my name. I would probably need to use a male pseudonym to sign my work.

Were it not for conflicts, I would not vote either, and would still be seen first as my father's property, then my husband's.

If there was no conflict, black people would still be enslaved; the culture of native peoples would not be seen as legitimate, not to talk about the demarcation of their territory; there would be no agrarian reform; LGBTQIA+ people would not be able to marry and adopt children... Just imagine the structural violence and sameness of a world without conflict!

So, I invite you to repeat it with me, and to do it again and again - as much as it takes - until it sinks in: conflicts cannot be prevented! Restorative Justice doesn't seek to prevent conflicts!

On the contrary, the main interest of restorative practices in the face of conflicts is transformation. It is true that, in some cases, one may choose to resolve or even manage conflicts. This happens for reasons linked to the context and interests of the participants.

However, it is important to keep in mind that Restorative Justice offers great potential for transforming conflicts. This is because restorative practices are oriented toward solving concrete problems and working on the structure of relationships – in order to improve the conditions of the present and build a future that better addresses the needs of all stakeholders.

It is guided by ancestry, since it is based on various culturally established rituals around the globe. These rituals were brought together under the name of "restorative justice[28]", with the term

---

[28] The term "restorative justice" is subject to several criticisms. One of the main ones is precisely the one that concerns communities marked by trauma, which do not have a past that they want to restore - they want to build new bonds

becoming better known at the end of the last century from the efforts of the scholar Howard Zehr[29].

Restorative practices can be applied in any type of conflict, as long as the interested parties show interest and willingness.

Although they can be materialized in a myriad of forms – totally or partially restorative – their most common rituals usually include individual and collective encounters, along with follow-up sessions.

Even if all these steps are possible and relevant, RJ can be practiced without collective meetings. It is a mistake to assume that restorative

---

and ways of connecting. In that context, it is important to look at the term with the same generosity that restorative justice invites us to look at the other and at ourselves: seeking to understand its most adequate meaning, its best self. Zehr himself comments that Restorative Justice is not completed solely with the restoration of a previous ideal situation but in the construction of new conditions and possibilities for more humanized bonds between those involved.

[29] Cf. Zehr, Howard. (2015). *Changing lenses*: restorative justice for our times. (Twenty-fifth-anniversary edition). Herald Press.; Zehr, Howard; Van Acker, Tônia (trad.). (2012). *Justiça restaurativa*. Palas Athena.

practice becomes complete only through group encounters.

On the contrary, in several cases, collective meetings may not be necessary or even desired – and making an adequate practice demands one to take care of variables like these.

Another striking feature of RJ is the construction of its space with elements that promote connection, starting with the encouragement of a circular disposition of the participants.

In this regard, it is important to re-emphasize that Restorative Justice is not to be confused with the peace-building circle, and that it is possible that a practice that formally covers the structure of circular processes step-by-step is not restorative.

As highlighted in the previous chapter, for a process to be considered restorative, there are a number of practices that can be applied with a certain degree of flexibility and adaptability to the problematic situation at stake, but it has to carry a consistent structure of principle.

Its biggest differentiator is the participation not only of those directly involved in the case, but also of those indirectly interested, either because they compose the support and referral network of the direct participants, or because they have a subsidiary relationship with what happened.

Not every restorative practice involves a current conflict, it may be aimed at preventing future problems or even at stimulating connection between the participants – working on issues such as belonging; understanding different perspectives on a challenging topic; strengthening bonds; reinserting someone who was away from the community back into it; creating support groups or sharing experiences; promoting memory and learning; establishing standards of conduct or sharing responsibilities regarding their observance; celebrating or mourning; and welcoming.

Restorative practices can have purposes as diverse as the needs of those involved! This is a great differentiator of restorative justice: it must adapt to the human community, not the other way around. Therefore, the malleability of its procedures.

However, some elements and principles must be observed in order to ensure the conduct of its practices, which can be totally or partially restorative as they integrate these components.

A fully restorative practice is one that responds with maximum efficiency to the following questions: a) does the method fully contemplate the needs, possible damages, and the causes of the problematic situation?; b) does it adequately address people who have had their needs affected, who suffered or who are suffering harm or threats to their rights?; c) are people encouraged to take active responsibility?; d) are the stakeholders being considered, and have they been included in practice?; e) have the micro-communities of support and referral been mobilized?; f) are there opportunities for substantial dialogue, with active speaking and listening, and participatory decision-making?; g) are those involved being respected and considered in their individualities?

Just as an example, I will list some of the places where conflicting situations appear and in which — if there is voluntariness — the restorative practice is possible: family, societal, school, neighborhood, and workplace conflicts, involving workgroups or coexistence.

In addition, it is possible there to be restorative practices both in the face of inter-individual conflicts and in more complex cases with environmental and labor collective conflicts, for example.

2.1 Micro-community and conflict transformation

During the time I lived in Palestine, I've had the opportunity of working with *The Friends School*, in Ramallah. Even though this school is driven by Non-Violent Communication, conflicts in the school environment remain constant. The difference isn't in the plane of existence, but how they deal with conflicts when they happen[30].

One time, I witnessed a conflict between two boys about seven or eight years old. One of them had made an unpleasant "joke" about the other's voice during class. Two other students in the class immediately suggested that a circle be

---

[30] Halaby, Mona Hajja. (2000). *Belonging: creating community in the classroom*. Brookline Books.

made so that everyone had a chance to talk about how they felt.

Although the conflict happened directly between the two boys, they understood that the whole class had some share of responsibility and involvement in it. Social behavior is learned: we think not only through our language but also in accordance with symbolic behavior and power[31].

If that boy's mental structure authorized him to be violent with his colleague, it is because the usual codes of conduct in that community made this behavior possible, even if to condemn him. Not only that: if the other boy's voice was the object of demerit, it is because some value present in that space evaluated people positively or negatively based on this characteristic.

The conflict is social, territorial, and temporally demarcated. For this reason, it is always possible to promote change in the

---

[31] Bourdieu, Pierre. (2012). *O poder simbólico*. Bertrand Brasil.

relationship between the participants or in some of them individually, but conflict also carries with it the potential to promote true social transformation[32].

In this case, the programmed content for the class was interrupted due to the emergence of this new fact. Everyone present – the students and the teacher – participated in the circle, since, to some extent, everyone was affected by what had happened. Belonging and the feeling of being in a safe and respectful space are directly influenced by the environment. It was important for each of them that that classroom was a place of interdependence and cooperation.

In addition, albeit indirectly, everyone had taken part in the conflict. The environment impacts the development of conflicts. More

---

[32] Cf. Holman, Peggy. (2010). *Engaging emergence: turning upheaval into opportunity*. Berret Koehler.; Holman, Peggy. (1999). *The change handbook: group methods for shaping the future*. Berret Koehler.; United Nations Development Programme. (2007). *Democratic Dialogue: a handbook for practitioners*. International Idea.

constructive or more destructive environments affect not only the existence but also the escalation level of conflicts[33].

In the circle, each participant had the opportunity to briefly talk about how they felt regarding what had happened and how they believed they could contribute to building a class that better welcomed its members. Those directly involved were also able to talk about how they had been impacted and what they needed.

In a few minutes, not only the situation had been resolved, but the micro-community's bonds had been strengthened. Meaning and belonging went back to being elements present in that space. The class had learned something new about themselves and sought to transform their

---

[33] Deutsch, Morton. (1986). Cooperation, Conflict, and Justice. In.: Bierhoff, Hans Wermer; Cohen, Ronald; Greenberg, Jerald. (Eds.). *Justice in Social Relatio.ns.* (pp. 3-18) Melvin J. Lerner.; Deutsch, Morton. (2014). Cooperation, competition, and conflict. In.: Coleman, Peter; Deutsch, Morton; Marcus, Eric. (Eds.). (pp. 3-28). *The handbook of conflict resolution: theory and practice.* Jossey-Bass.

values and relationships. Then, the teacher went back to teaching the programmed content, now with more attention from the students.

Following this same paradigm, the University of Turku, Finland – with funding from the country's Ministry of Education and Culture – developed the KiVa Program, which aims to combat, monitor, and prevent bullying in schools[34].

Kiva has been producing effective results precisely by mobilizing the affected micro-communities, extending the approach to conflict beyond the traditional notions of offender and victim, and reaching other central people such as those who offer support for the individual or group that has suffered the harm; the positive people of reference to the individual or group that have caused the harm; and also the people who

---

[34] Kiva International. *Evidence of effectiveness in Finland and elsewhere.* Kiva Program. https://www.kivaprogram.net/kiva-is-effective/.

have supported the existence of this harm – be it by smiling, by encouraging it or by being silent.

Within these approaches, conflict is no longer viewed exclusively as a risky situation, it also becomes an opportunity to promote substantial change.

According to Deutsch, "conflict prevents stagnation, stimulates interest and curiosity, it is the medium through which problems can be aired and solutions arrived at. It is the root of personal and social change[35]". It also demarcates groups, helps to establish collective and individual identities, and, when external, can contribute to internal cohesion.

When conflicts occur, it is only possible to respond to the immediate situation. However, focusing exclusively on emergencies can distract the gaze from what is important. An enlarged map

---

[35] Deutsch, Morton. (2004). A resolução do conflito. In: Azevedo, Andre Gomma de. (Ed.). *Estudos em arbitragem, negociação e mediação.* (pp. 29-44). UNB.

of the conflict also involves understanding the causes and forces present; the patterns of the relationships at stake; the context in which it is expressed; and the conceptual framework that supports these perspectives[36].

Therefore – within a broader view that considers the topography of the problematic situation – the conflict emerges as an opportunity to understand the patterns and modify the structures of relationships. Without, of course, disregarding the need to offer concrete solutions capable of responding satisfactorily to present problems.

It is also an effective way to conduct large public discussions about the heart of issues and relationships that are usually confined to the private sphere.[37]. Thus, conflicts can be an important way to stimulate reflection and deepen

---

[36] Lederach, John Paul. (2012). *Transformação de conflitos.* Palas Athena.
[37] Braithwaite, John. (2006). Doing Justice Intelligently in Civil Society. *Journal of Social Issues*, 62(2), pp. 393-409.

the understanding of the context, structure, and patterns of relationships' implications in issues that appeared before to be merely interpersonal.

To map a conflict, it is important to pay attention to at least the following elements: the characteristics of the subjects involved, as well as their interests and needs; the power structures and patterns of intersubjective relationships; the conceptual frameworks that support each of these perspectives; the world views of the individuals and groups involved; and the emotions aroused by the conflict situation[38].

Here, peace is a *structure-process*[39], always dynamic, relational, adaptive, and purposeful. It is sustainable – being able to maintain itself over time, despite the eventual structural rigidity.

---

[38] Calvo Soler, Raúl. (2014). *Mapeo de conflictos: técnica para la exploración de los conflictos*. Gedisa.
[39] Lederach, John Paul. (2012). *Transformação de conflitos*. Palas Athena.

With this scenario in mind, it is possible to take action to effectively and profoundly – besides solving current and specific problems – understand the patterns and modify the structures of relationships[40].

For this, it is essential to facilitate the creation and strengthening of links of meaning within these practices. That is, the perception that the dialogues established there are significant, that all voices are considered in the decision-making process, and that the listening process is based on reciprocity.

Being conscious of the impact of taking individual narratives into account also brings a sense of belonging, feeding back into the very notion of community itself.

This dialogue process, by basing itself on the creative power of collective knowledge, does not necessarily guarantee control of the results –

---

[40] Lederach, John Paul. (2012). *Transformação de conflitos*. Palas Athena.

but it fosters the perception that every person's voice is important in that space.

The identification of a safe space for building involvement, support, reciprocity, and transformation is based on the sensible difference between simply speaking and being listened to.

For social transformation to happen, rather than joining countless voices that point in the same direction together, it is important to maintain diversity and representation within the dialogic spaces. What must be sought is not unanimity in decisions, or *coercive harmony*[41], but the permanence of dialogue so that there is adequate space for building perspectives as complete and complex as possible.

The constancy of dialogue is understood as a metabolic process of community life. Since community is bigger than the sum of its parts,

---

[41] Nader, Laura, (1994). *Harmonia coercitiva: a economia política dos modelos jurídicos*. Revista Brasileira de Ciências Sociais, 9 (26). https://anpocs.com/images/stories/RBCS/26/rbcs26_02.pdf.

continuous movement is essential to the collective existence: like everything alive, it flows – *pant rei*[42]. This intentionality is a significant part of steady learning, and the creation and strengthening of the monitoring and dialogue channels' adaptability networks.

Connection through the reciprocal sharing of perspectives, needs, and vulnerabilities in a safe space strengthens those involved and awakens the potential for creative life.

If problems are not correctly named, the alternatives imagined for overcoming them are unlikely to be effective. Just as chemotherapy does not cure measles, choosing the appropriate treatment demands an identification of the problematic situation as precisely as possible.

This perspective considers the human condition not a problem, but a solution. It is for our shared humanity and continuous dialogue that

---

[42] Ephesus, Heraclitus of. (2013). *Heráclito: los fragmentos*. Laodamia Press.

it is possible to establish *moral imagination* and creative social transformation.

2.2 Narrativity and being otherly in conflict

Perhaps the greatest impact of restorative practice on conflicts is precisely the fact that, even when focused on them, RJ does not confuse the participants with the conflict itself. That is: although centered on conflict, it is not exclusively focused on it.

That's why, in Instituto Pazes[43] we say that we may receive cases, but we work with people.

---

[43] It is common for peace to be thought of as calmness and silence. With legal academic training and experience in research and practice in conflict transformation, Elaine Cristina, Lucas Jerônimo and Mayara Carvalho believed that it was essential to spread an idea of peace full of voices and diversity. "Peaces" (Pazes, in the original), in the plural, just as people are. That's how Instituto Pazes was born, born from these three facilitators' dream of contributing to "making peaces" ("fazer as pazes", in portuguese) among humanity –

Remember what we said before about the danger of the single story. Often, in conflicts, the only story the people involved know about each other is their involvement in the situation, which may then be confused by them with the identification of polarization.

In RJ, something that helps participants see other people in their humanity is the fact that they have contact with stories about each of the other people involved from outside of the conflict. Stories narrated by their protagonist. Stories that bring more than opposite poles, precisely because they show human beings. With this, RJ intends to

---

building more just, egalitarian, meaningful connections that foster active responsibility.

After years of work and research in the areas of access to justice, human and fundamental rights and restorative methodologies based on the transformation of conflicts, the foundation of an Institute comes from the objective of joining efforts for the permanent study and qualification of all people interested in facilitating actions and projects with justice and restorative practices, Nonviolent Communication, conflict resolution and transformation, community development, and integrative and systemic practices associated with personal and professional development.

Cf. www.pazes.com.br

stimulate the perennial openness to the other – being *otherly*[44].

As presented by Levinas, the adverb *otherly*, from the French *l'autrement*, is guided by the ethics of alterity, through the contact between the individual and the other – different from them. That is, it is not the proximity, but the difference that is the main mark of justice and the humanization of relationships.

I borrow Levinas' concept to present it within the restorative paradigm, defending that the visibility of difference in the present is essential, "[...] an inter-est, an inter-estment – which marks the triumph, and not the subversion of being[45]".

For RJ's vision of justice as the satisfaction of needs, justice is materialized precisely in the

---

[44] Levinas, Emmanuel. (2014). *Violência do rosto*. Loyola.
[45] Ricoeur, Paul. (2008). *Outramente: leitura do livro Autrement qu'être ou au- delà de l'essence de Emmanuel Lévinas*. Vozes. p.19.

awareness and visibility of difference in the here and now.

It also recognizes that treating a person with inhumanity violates the very concept of humanity and, therefore, even if you don't realize it, it affects all human beings, not just the group directly made vulnerable[46].

It's also in this sense that Fanon defends that "All forms of exploitation are identical because all of them are applied against the same 'object': man [...] I can't help but be solidary with my brother's fate[47]".

In Levinas' words,

---

[46] Cf. Segato, Rita Laura. (2006). Antropologia e direitos humanos: alteridade e ética no movimento de expansão dos direitos universais. *MANA*, 12(1). pp.207- 236.; Segato, Rita Laura (2003). La argamassa jerárquica: violencia moral, reproducción del mundo y la eficácia simbólica del Derecho. In.: Segato. (2006). Rita Laura. *Las estructuras elementales de la violencia: ensayos sobre género entre la antropologia, el psicoanálisis y los derechos humanos.* Universidad Nacional de Quilmes.

[47] Fanon, Frantz. (1967). *Black Skin, White Masks.* Grove Press.

> I have always described the face of the neighbor as the bearer of an order which imposes on the self which faces the other a free – and inalienable responsibility as if the self was chosen and unique – and the other man is absolutely other, that is, still incomparable and thus unique[48].
> *[free translation]*

The philosopher presents dialogue as a communicative modality from which the individual is able to think more than they think, since, through it, thought extrapolates what's given: the individual surpasses their – limited by the opportunities and experiences already known to them – universe and reaches a fragment of the other's particular world.

Being in contact with difference makes the being more than what they were – or what they were until the opportunity for communication in the face of difference.

---

[48] Levinas, Emmanuel. (2014). *Violência do rosto.* Loyola. p. 28.

Dialogue is conducted through active listening and speech directed to the other, not through the exercise of tutelage or through speaking for the other[49]. Being *otherly*, therefore, is an important step in the way to understanding the human being as a totality – that is, as part of everything that exists, following an ethics of responsibility regarding other beings and the planet.

In this sense, Sartre[50], Fanon[51], James Baldwin[52], and many others have affirmed, each in their context, that it is the supremacist who creates the relationships of inferiorization and the image of the inferiorized. Baldwin goes even further, stating that until we understand the reason that led white to create the image of black,

[49] Spivak, Gayatri Chakravorty. (2014). *Pode o subalterno falar?*. Editora UFMG.
[50] Sartre, Jean-Paul. (1985). *Réflexions sur la question juive*. Paris Gallimard.
[51] Fanon, Frantz. (1967). *Black Skin, White Masks*. Grove Press.
[52] Peck, Raoul (Director). (2016). *I am not your Negro* [Film]. Velvet Film; Artemis Productions; Close Up Films.

we will not be able to recapture the human condition that unites all of us.

Similarly, Fanon narrates,

> I came into this world anxious to uncover the meaning of things, my soul desirous to be at the origin of the world, and here I am an object among other objects.
>
> **Locked in this suffocating reification, I appealed to the Other so that his liberating gaze, gliding over my body suddenly smoothed of rough edges, would give me back the lightness of being I thought I had lost, and taking me out of the world put me back in the world. But just as I get to the other slope I stumble, and the Other fixes me with his gaze, his gestures, and attitude, the same way you fix a preparation with a dye.** I lose my temper, and demand an explanation. Nothing doing. I explode. Here are the fragments put together by another me.
>
> **As long as the black man remains on his home territory, except for petty internal quarrels, he will not have to experience his being for others.** here is in fact a "being for

> other," as described by Hegel, but any ontology is made impossible in a colonized and acculturated society. [...] For **not only must the black man be black; he must be black in relation to the white man. [...]The black man has no ontological resistance in the eyes of the white man.** From one day to the next, the Blacks have had to deal with two systems of reference. Their metaphysics, or less pretentiously their customs and the agencies to which they refer, were abolished because they were in contradiction with a new civilization that imposed its own.[53].
> *[emphasis added]*

This encounter between different beings, even if it is prospective and if it carries memories and ancestry, is constructed in the present, regarding the current beings, which is why it is always provisory, just like the ephemeral here-now.

---

[53] Fanon, Frantz. (1967). *Black Skin, White Masks.* Grove Press.

> [...] Every human problem cries out to be considered on the basis of time, the ideal being that the present always serves to build the future.
> And this future is not that of the cosmos, but very much the future of my century, my country, and my existence. In no way is it up to me to prepare for the world coming after me. I am resolutely a man of my time.
> And that is my reason for living. The future must be a construction supported by man in the present. This future edifice is linked to the present insofar as I consider the present something to be overtaken.[54].

Perhaps this is what Fanon means when he says that

> Here is my life caught in the noose of existence. Here is my freedom, which sends back to me my own reflection. No, I have not the right to be black.
> It is not my duty to be this or that....

---

[54] Fanon, Frantz. (1967). *Black Skin, White Masks.* Grove Press.

[...] I find myself one day in the world, and I acknowledge one right for myself: the right to demand human behavior from the other.

And one duty: the duty never to let my decisions renounce my freedom.

I do not want to be the victim of the Ruse of a black world

[...] I am not a prisoner of History. I must not look for the meaning of my destiny in that direction.

I must constantly remind myself that the real leap consists of introducing invention into life.

In the world I am heading for, I am endlessly creating myself.

I show solidarity with humanity provided I can go one step further.

[...] I am not a slave to slavery that dehumanized my ancestors.

[...] There should be no attempt to fixate man, since it is his destiny to be unleashed.

The density of History determines none of my acts.

I am my own foundation.

[...] **I, a man of color, want but one thing:**

May man never be instrumentalized. May the subjugation of man by man. — that is to say, of me by another—cease. May I be

allowed to discover and desire man wherever he may be.
[...] Why not simply try to touch the other, feel the other, discover each other?
[...] My final prayer:
O my body, make me always a man who questions![55]

2.3 Security and citizenship: breaking with the single-story in polarized conflicts

In the country with the most deaths by firearms in the world[56], one wonders how much of our dictatorship remains in our democracy[57].

If one analyses the circumstances of the police presence in Brazilian suburbs, it is possible to find many similarities between the actions

---

[55] Fanon, Frantz. (1967). *Black Skin, White Masks*. Grove Press.
[56] Travisan, Maria Carolina. *O Brasil é o país que mais mata por arma de fogo no mundo*. Flacso Brasil. http://flacso.org.br/?publication=o-brasil-e-o-pais-que-mais-mata-por-arma-de-fogo-no-mundo.
[57] Cf. Jupiara, Aloy; Otavio, Chico. (2015). *Os porões da contravenção: jogo do bicho e ditadura militar: a história da aliança que profissionalizou o crime organizado*. Record.

portrayed in the documentary "Santa Marta: duas semanas no morro" (Santa Marta: two weeks in the slum), directed by Eduardo Coutinho[58] at the end of the last Brazilian dictatorship with the destiny of mason assistant Amarildo Dias de Souza, disappeared since July 2013 after being detained by the Military Police; or even of Marielle Franco, former Rio de Janeiro Councilwoman and a critic of the Police's performance in the favelas, brutally murdered in March 2018.

However, one must take care not to fall into the danger of the single-story regarding the trajectory of the Brazilian Military Police. At Nacional, as I observed during my Ph.D.'s empirical research, a considerable part of the *Security with Citizenship* Project's results came from the partnership built between the community and the Military Police, under Major Davidson Tavares's local command.

---

[58] Coutinho, Eduardo (Director). (1987). *Santa Marta: duas semanas no morro*. [Documentary] Ministério da Justiça.

Davidson, then Lieutenant, joined the Local Committee at the invitation of the Nacional's residents. Davidson Tavares' relationship with the community had not always been close: both parties seemed to be guided by a single story about the other.

A change in perspective is reported by Claudia Ocelli – the Municipality of Contagem's Focal Point in the Joint UN Program – in her statement:

> Before the Program, Lieutenant Davidson referred to the boys as "thugs". [...] When community policing was implemented, they did training with Beto from Papo de Responsa in Rio de Janeiro. After it, the Lieutenant changed so radically that, in one of the Local Committee meetings, he was very sad when he started his speech, saying that he had done a Police Report of the 'son of my great friend' and that he had not been able to do anything to turn this situation around, and that he had learned the week before

that the teen had been sworn to death.

Cintia Yoshihara, who was United Nations Development Programme's consultant on Security with Citizenship from 2010 to 2013, reports that, from the community's perspective, the opening to different narratives about the Military Police came from a speech by Major Davidson at a Committee meeting. By exposing the vulnerability and difficulties of the Police's working conditions in the territory, he made the community empathetic to the human beings who wore the Police uniform.

In Major's words:

> [The trust invested in me by nomination for the Local Committee came because] there was a time lag between the arrival of this UN project and the work we had already started there. I was in the territory all day long; I practically didn't stay at the Headquarters. [...] **We would park the vehicle around the neighborhood, and it wasn't**

just repression, it wasn't just approaching people and seeing who had drugs and who hadn't. There, we would park the vehicle around the square, go to the local businesses on foot; talk to a shopkeeper, talk with another; I used to go to the health center, talk.. **People started to greet us, to know who we were.** And they knew it like this: 'that person is the commander, who is taking care of here and **they knew that we were really focused on promoting community safety - that we were not concerned with repression only.** [We were] concerned with safety in general: if [repression] had to happen, it would. At first, it was about this: generating a sense of safety for them with our presence, an idea that we were going to reverse this whole situation. On a daily basis, if there was a party, we were there; at the meeting, we were present. **[Even] it if was a meeting that was not related to public safety, if it was something they thought was important, we attended.** So, they got to take their time to recognize that we really had a different way of doing the job. *[emphasis added]*

The Major's relationship with the community was so close that only one of the civilians interviewed in my field research did not directly allude to the Policeman's name. Likewise, although away from the territory since the end of the Joint Program, Davidson Tavares remembered the names and narratives of the community leaders.

In an interview, community leader Zé Gordo[59] narrated that

> We would like for people to think about it again [about leisure for our youth], understanding the way young people think. As we saw Lieutenant Davidson, who used to take one thing from here, another from there [to donate to children in the community], do. He even once came to my house

---

[59] José Ferreira de Souza, known as "Zé Gordo", community leader who participated on the joint proposal of the *Security with Citizenship*'s activities, and then on their implementation in the territory.

to get a little gift, and then went to the community and shared it with the children. **This is what we wanted to see from our Police: not letting young people be afraid of it, but to be a Police Force connected to the youth.** [...] Sometimes a boy passes by, and if there's a policeman in the street, he already runs away in fear. **And the Police are not meant to be feared, the Police are meant to be there, defending our rights**, right? And peace, which for me is a very important thing. I can only be thankful for what the UN has done here, and for my colleagues in the community, Marcos, Café, Tony Lanche, Café's sister, Raquel – who also worked – several people, and even people from the City Hall who were connected to it all... **we were together for the community**. *[emphasis added]*

The initiative that Zé Gordo was referring to in this quote is "Military Police Santa Claus", a project in which the policemen sponsored children in vulnerable situations, exchanging letters with the kids and offering them company and gifts during Christmas time.

At Nacional, "Military Police Santa Claus" was the result of a partnership between the Major and a community leader, Dona Penha, who maintained a community daycare center aimed at serving "children of poor people and even people with deviations", as highlighted by Davidson Tavares. As he only had from 10 to 15 workers at the Estrela Dalva Square, the Major extended the scope of the project, inviting officers from other regions to participate. As he narrated:

> During Christmas time, we went there, we took presents with us – this kind of things – we spent a good few hours with them, the little children. [...] We took the issue to the commander: our wish to do something different there, in that little school, at Dona Penha's daycare. And so, each policeman gave out some presents here. They had to write a little letter to us, you know? Each kid asked for something

different: some asked for a bicycle, others for a ball, but there were some who asked for food, school supplies...

The training offered by the UN was essential for this change of perspective about the link and relationship between the Police and the community. One of the courses, conducted by the actress Elisa Lucinda – creator of the project "Palavra de Polícia – Outras Armas" (Police Word – Other Weapons), sought to use poetry as a disarmament tool by using words to foster self-esteem, creativity, and self-knowledge.

Within the Joint Program, this initiative was intended to foment integration between the various actors who interacted with the territory, to make dialogue an instrument for the construction and strengthening of positive bonds within it.

Through poetry, the structuring of ideas and narratives was encouraged. Words, if carefully crafted, could claim rights, and talk about feelings and challenging issues, goals, and misunderstandings, without invading or disrespecting the other's space.

Talking about the project, Major Davidson commented that it was

> an art of using the verb, **using words to disarm, to converse, to reduce tension**. She [Elisa Lucinda] spent three days in the territory doing words work, a power-of-words work. Then, she gave a poem to each one of those present and ended the training on the Estrela Dalva Square, [where] each person had to recite the poem. And then we went to Brasília and stayed with her for two more days at a closing seminar for this training on the use of words, the power of words. She did a very good job, especially for those who stayed in the region. Those who stayed there and who needed to talk with all kinds of people, you know? [...] **We already understood a little about the use of progressive force in communication, about the need not to reach out by abruptly touching the person**. If you do

> this through dialogue... **but her technique of talking, of knowing how to connect the words, the intensity of each word according to the situation... made a difference.** I thought her work was very important for the whole community. *[emphasis added]*

Words were also decisive in another Police action at Nacional: the mapping of potential victims. Within it, there was the intelligence preventive action that sought to identify probable victims of homicide and prevent murders in the territory, caused mainly by drug trafficking. As Davidson Tavares warns, homicide "is the crime that generates the most insecurity. It is the crime that gives the region its character, especially among teenagers".

To do this mapping, then, the Military Police started to visit the potential victims' relatives' homes, to talk to the mothers and warn them about the seriousness of their situations.

Some cases were referred to witness protection programs, with the consequent removal of the threatened persons from the territory. In others, the dialogue and partnership with those responsible were enough to solve the situation, whether through reinforcement of care, dialogue with the teenager, or payment of debt.

In this case, the Policeman was emphatic in pointing out the significant decrease in homicides of adolescents at Nacional. As he alerted:

> Often, for society in general, the person who is dying is nothing more than a criminal. But this person is someone who has a mother, who has a father, who has a family, who has someone who likes them. Not only that, but these numbers also affect the community, and the city... it all adds up and generates a factor of insecurity. [...] sometimes this information came from the Police Intelligence itself, sometimes from a resident of the territory.

I don't know if you've heard of one of them, the one whose nickname is Café. He was a guy that the Police sometimes had as a criminal informer, sometimes as a Police informer. Some policemen didn't want anything to do with him because he had a good relationship with the people there, with the offenders. But we made use of it, we had the know-how. We used to go to his house, have breakfast with him, and enter the community with him, you know? Because there were times, in some situations, we had helped him. Like, not with crime... let's suppose, if it were up to Command, there wouldn't be a *baile funk* there that week, they didn't want it at all. And it turns out that we, being there, with his requests of 'ah, Lieutenant, give me a hand, at least a little... We used to say 'look, Café, if you do the *baile* and it doesn't end too late, or generate complaints, I won't have the police end it'. With this, he got a bargain. People already knew that sometimes he would talk to us, then someone would say to him, 'ah, Café, they're going to overtime on the guy...', using their lingo, because they also knew that maybe he was going to talk to us. And then everything was anticipated. **With that, we were there for a long time without any police reports.** These people... they have a lot of information. 'The Police are coming around more; the Police want to catch the murderer'. **Because it's very common for the homicide [of teenagers] to be registered and then abandoned – because the one who died was a delinquent. They already knew that we were going to go after it.** If there was a homicide, we would investigate it, we would try to find out who did it. And now the guy doesn't want to sign the Police Report. **He's a drug dealer, he's there, but the homicide Police Report... that he doesn't want to sign. He knows it'd be too heavy. Once he's in the system, he's smashed, let's put it like this.** [...] **And when there was a prison not made by us, a specialized battalion received a complaint and went there and took a bunch of stuff... The guy who lost the stuff is already a potential victim because he's not the trap house, he's not the dealer, he just had the material to be sold, he won't be able to pay and sometimes he will have done**

> **even more.** Sometimes, besides losing the drugs, we'll have given something more. So, we already knew... when we caught the Police Report, the other day, we already knew, that one guy had... *[emphasis added]*

In this community dialogue process, the Police began to identify which leaders could become important allies in building a safer neighborhood. It was in this context that the Major formed a closer relationship with the community leaders responsible for youth engagement through the Recanto da Pampulha (Pampulha's Nook) football team. It was through this partnership that he proposed the aforementioned "problem teenager"'s engagement as an administrator of the football field.

This involvement with community members helped in the protection of children and adolescents, but also of the policemen themselves – who then began to suffer less resistance from residents and had direct help from leaders who were now "less exposed, without direct contact with the face of public security in the territory", as highlighted by the Major.

This connection ended up directly interfering with the collective image of violence at Nacional and its possible solutions. So much so that the Police began to work with the Department of Education to investigate how school dropouts and teenagers' involvement in legal infractions or vulnerable living conditions were linked.

About the issue, Major Davidson said:

> Once, while working, I came across a boy who must have been eight years old, and a girl, his sister, who must have been seven. I crossed paths with them, right there, digging through the garbage, playing in the garbage, rummaging through things. Then, I went looking for their parents. I went looking and found out that **the kids had been**

out of school for almost a year […] **I went to talk to their mother.** She was very scared, but we told her that our intention was just to solve the problem, so we talked to the Regional Administrator and the School's Principal, and worked it out to find a place for them there, you know? And through that, **we noticed the problem of school dropout rates was influencing the kids' involvement in violence there. And that started to make us worried. We made these referrals, brought up the topic in the meetings - so that it could be worked on along with the Department of Education so that this school dropout data could be collected – and we proposed that, if necessary, we would tag along – one way or another – in uniform or not, to check out what was going on.** […] After almost two years there, we noticed a big difference between boys who were under 12 years old and those who were over 12 years old. They completely lost their identity, the boys who used to greet us started to dislike the police, they changed their behavior and started to be influenced by the offenders, they lost their space

> at home and everything. I don't know to what extent they started to go out to the street more, and that was what influenced them and made them lose their innocence, their path. We realized how difficult it was to get them back, to fight this. Then, Paulinho [Terrinha] had this *graffiti* project, created with the intention to integrate lots of teens so that they could be trained there. [...] When we find people like this, Zé Gordo, Café, and Dona Penha, we get closer and closer and, thank God, I was very happy with them, and they liked us. Precisely because we came with the intention of helping. In whatever we could help, we helped. *[emphasis added]*

In this movement, the Police's actions in response to violence and security issues began to move closer to Zé Gordo's goal of offering leisure to promote social peacemaking. Thus, in addition to direct action with schools and the football team, they also started to support festivities and cultural events in the community, such as *bailes funk* and Severina Chic Chic's Saint John's feast.

This way, the meaning of security policy began to go along with that of citizenship. No wonder two other curfews that threatened the community were avoided even before being put in action.

The partnership between the Police and the community reinforced the possibility of creating dialogue and connection through the common needs between two poles – which until then saw each other as antagonists.

The overcoming of the single-story, in this case, changed both Police's view of the neighborhood and the resident's view of the Police.

Even in polarized and historically violent contexts, conflict transformation is possible. A good place to start is by sharing personal narratives – which serve both to increase awareness of what position one occupies in a given conflict; and to understand the impacts, needs, and feelings of other persons involved in the situation.

By providing a safe and intentional space for the nonviolent sharing[60] of these narratives, Restorative Justice can do much to transform conflicts, relationships, and communities.

---

[60] Restorative Justice is not satisfied with the mere sharing of narratives. That is to say: it is not just about speaking, but how the narration is done. This is why RJ and Nonviolent Communication are so closely related. More on the subject in cf. Carvalho, Mayara; Jeronimo, Lucas; Silva, Elaine Cristina da. (2020). *Comunicação Não-Violenta: diálogos e reflexões*. Instituto Pazes.

3 RESTORATIVE JUSTICE AND/IN VIOLENCE

Although I said before that "conflict" is the most *mainstream* perspective of Restorative Justice's uses, the truth is that – given the historical confusion between the two terms – in fact, when speaking of conflict, people tend to think about restorative practices in cases of violence.

I want to emphasize this even more: it is common to associate the potential of Restorative Justice practices, in a reductionist way, with crimes or law infractions.

Several misconceptions may underlie this frequent error. Between their possible causes, I highlight: a) the recent emergence of conflictology as a science and the even more recent understanding that conflict is not, nor does it presume violence; b) the popularization of Howard Zehr[61]'s work on restorative justice, which deals with a vision of justice more specifically applied in the criminal and juvenile scopes; c) lack of knowledge of previous Restorative Justice application in humanitarian practices[62]; d) the usurpation of the use of self-composition as a form of *Macdonaldization* of access to justice for vulnerable groups[63].

Yes, Restorative Justice has a specific application in the face of violence, working to contribute both to its prevention and to the construction of peace. But its scope is much broader than that.

---

[61] Cf. Zehr, Howard. (2015). *Changing lenses: restorative justice for our times*. Herald Press.
[62] Gade, Christian B. N. (2018). "Restorative Justice": History of the Term's International and Danish Use. In.: Nylund, Anna; Ervasti, Kaijus; Adrian, Lin. (Eds.). *Nordic Mediation Research*. Springer.
[63] Carvalho, Mayara; Coelho, Juliana. (2018). Autocomposição judicial: o meio mais rápido e barato para a macdonaldização das decisões? Análise segundo o CPC que ama muito tudo isso. In.: Cordeiro, Juliana; Norato, Ester; Marx Neto, Edgard. *Novas tendências: diálogos entre direito material e processual*. D'Plácido.

To understand that, it is necessary to undo another misconception about RJ's practices in violent situations: It is quite common for people to have a limited perception in regards to the extent of violence in conflict situations, which could encompass much more. Perceptions like this are, at the same time, selective and biased.

When I say that Restorative Justice has great application potential in cases involving violence, I am referring not only to physical violence but also psychological violence; verbal or non-verbal; material or immaterial; real or virtual; cultural and structural; historical or episodic; circumstantial or ongoing; impersonal or motivated; deliberate or unintentional; internal and external; individual or collective; legitimate and illegitimate.

When I say that, I mean that Restorative Justice also has a place in situations where the violence is deeply rooted – such as historical, structural, and cultural harms.

In that sense, I also affirm that it is possible to work with RJ in cases involving intolerance or even hate crimes.

I speak too of the importance that the restorative process boosts reflection and awareness of violence down to gestures, onomatopoeia, gaze, and apathy.

In saying it this way, I'm talking not only about intentional violence but also of the numerous violent acts in our daily lives, done unintentionally, without us having any awareness of their practice.

And I say more: RJ does not deal only with the violence that a person or a group commits to another. For Restorative Justice, it is equally important to raise awareness and break cycles of internal violence that participants may be sustaining. The violence I direct to myself is also important to RJ!

Due to the spread of certain myths about restorative practices, it is quite common to hear that the foundations of RJ are harm, responsibility, and cooperation. From what we have discussed so far, I imagine you can see that if RJ does not presuppose violence – and much less harm – it would be extremely reductionist and incoherent for "harm" to be one of its foundations.

It is true that, when there are harms, Restorative Justice must seek to repair them. However, to assume that they are one of RJ's foundations is no less wrong just because it is commonplace.

This same observation can be applied to the alleged "restorative questions", which are frequently used generically, without the necessary knowledge that Howard Zehr presented each of them within the context of RJ practices in cases of violence.

Harm is not an essential element in conflicts, and even less in connection. It is important that I'm intentional and clear here too.

In the face of harm, the fundamental restorative questions will be: "Who has suffered or is suffering harm?", and "What does this person need?". In other words: What are their needs?; Who is responsible for meeting them?; What elements contributed to causing the harmful act?; Which other people would be interesting to have in the process?; What method or process is appropriate in this context?.

Note that the question about what method or process to use was the last one. That was no coincidence: in the restorative perspective, the choice of the method will only be properly done if, before being proposed, it considers all the information accounted for by the previous questions.

If the answer "circular processes", "restorative conferences" or even "mediation" comes out of the facilitator's mouth before they carefully listen to what those involved have to say about each of those questions, we are not working with a suitable method – since, if at all, they relied on chance or on their presuppositions about the case to assess the suitability of the chosen method.

Although I share the anguish regarding the difficulties in evaluating the quality and restorative potential of practices so diverse and different, it is important to consider that the concept of access to justice as the satisfaction of needs understands that Restorative Justice's "how-to" can only be assessed on a case-by-case basis, never in abstraction. Not without reason, RJ emerged first as practice, and only later as a theory.

Since a poorly executed restorative practice can cause even greater harm to the victims than the regular disregard from legal proceedings[64], there must be space for listening to the practice's impacts on the conflict and the lives of the participants.

While it is true that the official justice system does not usually consider the needs of those who have suffered harm, studies show that it is also true that victims leave many restorative justice programs less satisfied than other participants[65].

For this reason, one of the essential phases of any restorative practice is the monitoring phase. A good resource to determine whether access to justice has been properly guaranteed is the analysis of the practice's effectiveness.

---

[64] Sherman, Lawrence; Strang, Heather. (2007). *Restorative Justice: the evidence.* The Smith Institute.

[65] Braithwaite, John. (2002). Does restorative justice work? In.: *Restorative justice and responsive regulation.* (pp. 45-72). Oxford University Press.

From the victim's perspective, a restorative practice may be viable because: a) it is a less formal procedure, in which their needs and feelings matter; b) it ensures more information and clarity about the process and its results; c) it is guided by direct involvement in the conflict situation; d) it encourages respectful and fair treatment, taking the victim's feelings, pain and needs into account; and e) it aims at material and emotional restoration[66].

Likewise, the fact that it involves support and referral micro-communities is in itself valuable, regardless of the harm's impacts and the eventual reparation of them.

By offering all participants in the situation the opportunity to get involved and decide how to ensure that that community is safer, more caring,

---

[66] Cf. Braithwaite, John. (2002). Does restorative justice work? In.: *Restorative justice and responsive regulation.* (pp. 45-72). Oxford University Press.

and welcoming, the restorative practice already makes these bonds potentially more humanized.

In this context, research by Christine Parker suggests, for example, that the existence of restorative practices to address sexual harassment in the workplace can effectively generate the reduction of this type of violence[67].

Recall now the case from the school in Ramallah, Palestine, presented earlier, in which the child who caused the harm, the one who directly suffered its effects, as well as the other students in the class and the teacher who was in the room at the time participated. The participation of those indirectly involved in the conflict was fundamental to building a culture of peace in that environment.

---

[67] Parker, Christine. (1999). Public Rights in Private Government: Corporate Compliance with Sexual Harassment Legislation, *Australian Journal of Human Rights*, 6, 5(1), p. 159-193.
http://classic.austlii.edu.au/au/journals/AUJlHRights/1999/6.html.

In addition, the restorative practice opened the opportunity for them to act as supporters, reminding each other of the agreements, needs and feelings worked on.

The participation of people called into the process by those directly involved in the situation can also be essential for them to have support to execute and maintain the actions agreed upon during the practice. The mere participation of people apparently not affected by the case but who are listed as referencesthemselves by those directly involved serves as a reminder to participants that they are not alone, that other people care about them and their happiness.

This is even more important when the case to be worked on involves children and teenagers, since they are, under the Rule of Law, citizens in a special developmental condition (as guaranteed in Brazil by art. 3º of the Law 8.069/1990), with shared responsibility by the family, the school, the

State and the community for their socio-education (as states art. 227 of the Brazilian Constitution of 1988).

3.1 Accountability in Restorative Justice

A common myth about restorative practices is that they "go easy on" those who have done harmful acts. This myth has more to do with eventual preconceptions and ignorance from the speaker than with the restorative practices itself.

This often happens because of the association between punishment and accountability. In fact, RJ does not position itself within the poles of the punishment-reward dyad.

Although they have accountability as one of their central elements, restorative practices do not focus on the determination of guilt, nor do they seek to shame those who did the harmful act. They also do not treat the person who suffered the harm as a mere touchstone for the conduction of the process.

Within restorative practices, accountability is necessarily active, that is, it demands that one understands the effects of their actions, who they affected, and how.

The practices presuppose, therefore, the active listening of each participant's needs, feelings, and perceptions about the situation.

For effective accountability to exist, it is essential to have a complete and complex view of the issue, understanding how it affects each of the stakeholders. Only then it is possible to think of an action plan that aims to meet the human needs manifested by the situation and repair, as far as possible, the harms that may exist.[68].

---

[68] Cf. Mackay, Robert E. (2013). The nexus between rights and restorative justice: using a case example of an organization 'C' – the right – or moral and spiritual claim – to recognition. In.: Gravielides, Theo; Artinopoulou, Vasso. *Reconstructing restorative justice philosophy*. Ashgate Publishing Limited.

For there to be accountability, one must observe some elements: a) the recognition that their action caused harm, even if it wasn't intentional; b) the understanding of oneself as an agent who could have acted differently; c) the comprehension of the direct and indirect impacts of the act; d) the building a set of actions aimed at, as far as possible, repairing the harm caused; e) the identification of personal patterns of behavior that made the harmful action possible; f) the transformation of these patterns of behavior. Although the last two aspects are not necessarily present in the restorative meetings themselves, they are frequent derivations of this process.

The restorative practice starts from paradigmatic questions aiming to identify who suffered the harm, what are their needs, and who is responsible for meeting these demands. It understands that every harm is linked to obligations that must be adequate to the needs of the people involved. To this end, RJ actively listens to those who performed the act, those who suffered direct and indirect harm from it, and the members of the support and referral micro-communities invited into the practice by these individuals.

Its focus, therefore, is on meeting needs so as to improve the situation of the people and relationships at hand. Aiming to repair harms, RJ refers not only to the concrete ones but also to those of a symbolic nature. This movement considers the harms in a universal way, also seeking to provide restoration for harms suffered by the community and by the author of the act.

This is because, although RJ practices focus on accountability, they assume that normally a person only causes harm to another when they have an incorrect or incomplete understanding of reality or when they are in a situation of vulnerability or suffering.

Within this humanized understanding of justice centered on the participants, the reparation of harms is aimed at all those involved in the conflict situation and can promote social transformation[69].

It is also a bet on the human condition, breaking with perspectives that usually presuppose the distrust on the humanity of the other. With the use of active listening and taking account of the stakeholders, restorative practices seek to act concurrently with *Strategies for Trauma Awareness & Resilience* (STAR), since trauma is a propeller of conflict and violence.

Although trauma is not a requirement for restorative practice, it must be borne in mind that – being people-centered – RJ is informed by trauma and resilience.

---

[69] Zellerer, Evelyn. (2013). Realizing the potential of restorative justice. In.: Gravielides, Theo; Artinopoulou, Vasso. *Reconstructing restorative justice philosophy.* Ashgate Publishing Limited.

For this reason, it seeks to identify patterns of trauma and stress, that is, of tensional response, whether individual or collective, offered in reaction to events, cumulative or continuous facts, as a reflex of exhaustion or strenuous disturbance. This reaction can happen on a personal, historical, transgenerational, cultural, or structural level. Its presence violates the dignity of the person or group by generating disconnection and exhaustion[70].

The role of meeting and the strengthening of connections they promote is fundamental in building resilience – in building the ability to reestablish individual or collective harmony, in

---

[70] Notion of trauma built in the *Strategies for Trauma Awareness & Resilience – level 1* course, held in 2018 by the *Center for Justice and Peacebuilding* at *Eastern Mennonite University< t5/>*, in Harrisonburg, Virginia, USA, with professors Donna Minter and Ram Bhagat. Cf. Yoder, Carolyn E.; Barge, Elaine Zook. (2012). *Strategies for Trauma Awareness and Resilience: The Unfolding Story.* Center for Justice and Peacebuilding; Center for Justice and Peacebuilding. (2017). *Strategies for Trauma Awareness and Resilience: Level I Participant Manual.* Eastern Mennonite University.

order to promote adaptation, transformation, or creative action in the face of challenges.

The sharing of stories and the presence of the support and referral micro-community are intended to intensify the feeling of belonging and the sense of meaning – and so, promoting relief and strengthening bonds.

In this process, RJ aims to offer opportunities for inserting large public discussions into everyday life, in order to connect the deep and mundane in the participants' lives.

Not demanding abstract debates focused on the political or academic spheres, RJ aims instead to root relevant transformations in the everyday relationships between people. By awakening awareness of empathy, isonomy, non-violence, and consideration, it seeks to insert the sublime into the usual, to make the extraordinary something of the ordinary.

Since it contemplates intimate themes and narratives of vulnerability, Restorative Justice is guided by secrecy. Without it, the construction of a safe space for sharing would be hampered. Confidentiality is crucial for the existence of said space and must be emphasized and discussed widely in the establishment of the rules of conduct that will guide collective sessions in RJ practices.

The rules of confidentiality must concern not only matters that may seem compromising to the people involved, but also those that lead to personal admiration. The assumption is that it is up to the person who told the story to decide to whom, how, when, and where their narrative can be spread. If the person who owns the story did not expressly consent to the dissemination of their narrative in a given external space, telling it would generate a breach of trust, even if done with good intentions.

Restorative practices enable and demand engagement from the parties affected or possibly affected by the issue, encouraging them to play significant roles in the decision-making process and in understanding the situation. They also encourage sharing narratives through the telling of stories that bring people together and present plots diverse from those exclusively linked to the problematic situation.

Participation is substantial, since restorative practices are built from each of the interested parties' narratives taking part in their collective knowledge[71].

As it seeks to transform the situation, RJ turns to the consequences and the causes of the problem, trying to undo injustices or inequalities on which the bonds between the people involved

---

[71] Pranis, Kay. (2010). *Processos circulares*. Palas Athenas; Pranis, Kay; Stuart, Barry; Wedge, Mark. (2003) Circles: a paradigm shift in how we respond to crime. In.: _____. *Peacemaking* circles: from conflict to community. Living Justice Press.

may be based; and seeking to repair other situations of vulnerability to which the participants are subjected.

RJ understands that punishment and victimization complement each other and, therefore, it seeks to move away from both. It understands that any attempt to control the behavior of others, either by discouragement or reward, is dehumanizing.

Restorative justice seeks, on the contrary, to broaden each of the participants' awareness so they understand the different causes, factors, consequences, and perspectives involved in the situation at hand. It also seeks to offer a safe space and an expanded landscape to carefully welcome and treat individual and collective traumas.

As mentioned before, for all this to be possible, it is essential that those involved express their willingness to participate in the restorative process, which should only continue up to when, where, and how they wish.

3.2 Restorative Justice, violence, and *moral imagination*

First of all, it is important to keep in mind that any community is a stage, a victim, and also a producer of violence[72]. That is, it is possible to identify violence in, by, and against the community – and that is directly related to the mental structures, the behavior patterns, the values, and the context in which said violence is inserted.

With knowledge of these dynamics, it's important to ask, then, how it would be possible

---

[72] Melo, M.B.P. (2013). (Re)pensar a violência escolar à luz das estratégias de intervenção em territórios de intervenção prioritária. In: Maria Manuel Vieira, José Resende, Maria Alice Nogueira, Juarez Dayrell, Alexandre Martins, António Calha (Eds.). *Habitar a escola e as suas margens: geografias plurais em confronto.* (pp. 157-169). Portalegre: Escola Superior de Educação, Instituto Politécnico de Portalegre.

to transcend the cycles of violence that permeate human communities while we remain living within them. To make this transcendence happen, it's necessary to mobilize the ability to create, use and build *moral imagination.*

For Lederach, *moral imagination* requires the ability to imagine ourselves in a relational network that includes the individuals we project as our enemies; the ability to sustain the curiosity that welcomes the complexity of life without falling back into polarization; the belief in the creative act and the pursuit for it; and the acceptance of the inherent risk of walking into the unknown that lies beyond the familiar scenarios of violence[73].

It demands, therefore, that we see beyond the visible reality to reach the hidden nature of relationships. The term *imagination* is not in the expression at random: the creative act is

---

[73] Lederach, John Paul. (2005). *The moral imagination: the art and soul of building peace.* Oxford University Press.

emphasized as a producer of new realities and a solution to old problems. The ability to create something original is a vector of change in the way situations and possibilities are seen.

By breaking with the superficial appearances that seemed to be decisive to build another possible future, this concept carries with it the quality of transcendence.

In Lederach's words,

> "The *moral imagination* is the capacity to imagine something rooted in the challenges of the real world yet capable of giving birth to that which does not yet exist. In reference to peacebuilding, this is the capacity to imagine and generate constructive responses and initiatives that, while rooted in the day-to-day challenges of violence, transcend and ultimately break the grips of those destructive patterns and cycles
> **This exploration does not push toward finding *the answer* to our problems in a single overarching solution, like some**

miraculous new political, social, or economic system. It does push us toward understanding the nature of turning points and how destructive patterns are transcended. Turning points are moments pregnant with new life, which rise from what appear to be the barren grounds of destructive violence and relationships. This unexpected new life makes possible processes of constructive change in human affairs and constitutes the moral imagination without which peacebuilding cannot be understood or practiced. However, such pregnant moments do not emerge through the rote application of a technique or a recipe. They must be explored and understood in the context of something that approximates the artistic process, imbued as it is with creativity, skill, serendipity, and craftsmanship". *[emphasis added]*[74]

---

[74] Lederach, John Paul. (2005). *The moral imagination: the art and soul of building peace.* Oxford University Press. p. 29.

Unlike violence, which assumes the lack of flexibility in creating more adequate solutions to respond to our problems, *moral imagination* comes from the ability to imagine ourselves as agents, as part of a relationship in which we want to welcome complexity and incorporate it into a creative act for constructive transformation.

Because it is based on creativity, it is an unforeseen act, an unexpected response created within each moment and, therefore, connected to the conscious presence in the present[75]. The moral imagination flows flexibly, observing the changes that emerge. As a complex, deep and creative movement, it is essentially based on simplicity, on the efficient, adapted, and reoriented use of the resources we have. Therefore, it connects intuition, attentive observation, and experience.

---

[75] Senge, Peter; et al. (2005). *Presence: exploring profound change in people, organizations and society.* Nicholas Brealey Publishing.; Machado, Regina. (2015). *A arte da palavra e da escuta.* Reviravolta.

According to the same author, "Art is what the human hand touches, shapes, and creates and in turn what touches our deeper sense of being, our experience. The artistic process has this dialectic nature: it arises from human experience and then shapes, gives expression and meaning to, that experience"[76].

Curiosity demands mindfulness[77] and continuous investigation into the things that surround us and their meanings. It is, in conclusion, both transcendental and mundane. No wonder, etymologically, curiosity comes from the Latin word *curiosus*, composed of the word for "care" and "healing" – *cura*. By considering what is *at the heart* of things, it escapes the danger of the

---

[76] Lederach, John Paul. (2005). *The moral imagination: the art and soul of building peace.* Oxford University Press. p. 51.

[77] Sabetti, Stèphano. (2015). *The path of no way: a spiritual primer: introduction to essential inquiry and process mediation.* Boston: Life energy media.; Tolle, Eckhart. (2010). *O poder do agora.* Sextante.

single story and seeks to heal and care for the health of greater humanity[78].

Practices disconnected from the natural flow of life that is creativity end up generating responses that aim to end harmful situations, instead of alternatives capable of building a desired future path. They focus more on reactive behavior than on active agency. Our historic inability to build democratic stability and lasting peace does not occur by chance[79].

---

[78] Levinas, Emmanuel. (1991). *Ética e infinito*. La balsa de la Medusa.; Estés, Clarissa Pinkola. (2017). *Women who run with the Wolves: myths and stories of the wild woman archetype*. River Wolf Press.

[79] Cf. Schwarcz, Lilia Moritz; Starling, Heloisa Murgel. (2015). *Brasil: uma biografia*. Companhia das Letras.

3.3 From narratives of violence to community transformation: the case of the Anne Frank Municipal School

As stated in the previous chapters, one of the forms of violence that exist in our world consists of starting a story with the second thing that happened.[80].

Imagine if you start the Confisco narrative as follows: Confisco is a poor neighborhood at the intersection of the municipalities of Belo Horizonte and Contagem. It is greatly affected by violence, with recurrent accounts of drug trafficking, homicide, aggression, domestic violence, and sexual abuse. Its streets are usually dirty, and the buildings are poorly maintained. It is common to find unaccompanied children on its streets.

Now, imagine a different situation. You've never directly heard of the neighborhood, and

---

[80] Adichie, Chimamanda Ngozi. (2009, October 7th). *The danger of the single story*. YouTube. https://www.youtube.com/watch?v=D9Ihs241zeg.

you've never been there. You don't have friends who were born or live at Confisco. Maybe you don't even know how to locate it on the city map. But now and then it appears to you as an element within shocking news.

Think of headlines like: "young man is brutally murdered in a street at Confisco", "drug dealer is found dead at Confisco", "murder at the Confisco neighborhood", "teen suspected of killing foreigner is apprehended at Confisco", "woman is murdered by her partner in front of Social Assistance Reference Center at Confisco".

All these stories, even if true, are partial cutouts. There was, once upon a time... and there wasn't, once upon a time[81]. All of this is "the second thing that happened". So, let's start a little earlier, let's go back about 30 years in the neighborhood's history.

---

[81] Cf. Estés, Clarissa Pinkola. (2017). *Women who run with the Wolves: myths and stories of the wild woman archetype*. River Wolf Press.

This time, imagine that I tell you what I reported in the first chapter's case study: Confisco was built with whatever resources its first residents managed to gather at the time, having arisen from the need for housing of about 160 families who lived in a squatting in the region, which was then a large estate. Except for the farmhouse, the first residences were made out of canvas and did not have water supply, electricity, sanitation, garbage collection, public transport, or paving. The garbage was discarded in one of the terrain's lower areas, known as "big hole", which led to the constant presence of rats, cockroaches, snakes, scorpions, and insects in the territory.[82].

---

[82] Data provided by the residents and by the Centro de Referência Popular do Bairro do Confisco (People's Reference Center of the Confisco Neighborhood). As for the latter, similar accounts can be accessed on the center's Facebook page. Cf.: Centro de Referência Popular do Bairro do Confisco. (2014, March 21) *Histórico do Conjunto Confisco*. Facebook. https://www.facebook.com/confiscobh/posts/hist%C3%B3ric o-do-conjunto-confiscoo-conjunto-confisco-nasceu-em-1988- e-est%C3%A1-localiza/440726819404942/..

In other words, Confisco began in a series of trials and tribulations. Its residents, however, persisted and articulated solidarity networks that sought to provide support to homeless families, report on opportunities and events, and prevent violence. Currently, there is a very active community network called "Confisco pela Paz" (Confisco for Peace). Besides that, the neighborhood's streets are now paved, and it is possible to get there by bus. The houses now have water and electricity supplies too.

Now imagine I tell you even more. I tell you that one of Brazil's 18 transforming schools[83] is located in Confisco. I add that it consists of a municipal public institution and that, in 2010, its activities were interrupted by a curfew that had been established in the region.

---

[83] Ashoka Brasil; Alana. *Escolas transformadoras: Sobre. Escolas Transformadoras.* http://escolastransformadoras.com.br/o-programa/sobre/.

I tell you too that a few years before, the school faced big challenges with drug trafficking, kids carrying guns around, and adults serving time invading the space to sexually abuse the students.

Imagine that I tell you that the connection between the school and the community built belonging within both; that I tell that, on Saturdays, residents of the neighborhood – be they students or not – play football in the institution's field, that the school's fairs happen on the streets, and the community is invited to participate.

Picture that I tell you even more: I tell you that students and teachers of this public schooling institution won international funding and went to Amsterdam to get to know more about Anne Frank's story. Think of your surprise to discover that these kids' creations were part of an exhibition in the Netherlands.

Would you believe me if I told you that the Anne Frank Municipal School's recent projects won a series of national and international human rights prizes? And if I introduced you to this school's extremely competent professionals that, besides their basic roles, work too on making dreams come through? If you got to know the History Teacher, Moacir Fagundes, the former Principal, Sandra Mara, the Arts Professor, Luciana, and the former History Interns, Luiza e Gislaine?

If I told you that, in 2016, the seventh year students, together with Professor Moacir and three interns, investigated the neighborhood's history and made a comic book telling the facts from the start. If I told you that this comic book was idealized by Maria das Graças Silva Ferreira, one of the neighborhood's founders, and strongly supported by the then Principal, Sandra Mara, as a vehicle to publicize alternative narratives about

Confisco – all of them true, but less known than the sensationalist headlines about violence. Would that change your image of Confisco?

A story is determined by the point from which it is told[84]. The neighborhood's image and its residents change significantly when the story is told starting from the first thing that happened. The partiality of the cutout can be even more damaging when it is presented as the definitive story as if it is the single existing story. And if this is done through the State, the epistemic violence takes on an official status and can produce high-impact harm and trauma.

If we focus the narrative on violence, powerlessness or on the lack of resources of a given group of people, for example, we establish a perspective that tends to teach through the production of trauma. On the contrary, the focus

---

[84] Adichie, Chimamanda Ngozi. (2009, October 7th). *The danger of the single story.* YouTube. https://www.youtube.com/watch?v=D9Ihs241zeg.

of the "Confisco pelo Confisco" (Confisco by/for Confisco) story is on protagonism and social transformation. I'll tell you what I heard from the community.

Once upon a time, not long ago, in a very distant neighborhood, there was a History Teacher named Moacir Fagundes who worked at a municipal school called Anne Frank. Moacir liked history and stories: the oral and the written, the told and the untold.

One day, while teaching the seventh-year students, he was interrupted by talking in the classroom. That's when he heard a student calling another "confisquer". And since when is birthplace a form of cursing? Since long, long ago, he knew; after all, he was a history teacher.

He could have just sighed and continued the class, but that made Moacir uneasy. Like Paulo Freire, he believed that "there is no true word that is not praxis. Hence, saying the true word transforms the world[85]".

Where he could have seen a mere act of indiscipline, the Teacher saw the students' shame in identifying themselves as residents of Confisco. He also noted that they preferred to say they lived "after the zoo" than naming their neighborhood.

How could he teach European history and ignore the history so close to him – a history that was already knocking on his door, before even being invited? But textbooks didn't teach it. The Ministry of Education seemed to ignore that, between Belo Horizonte and Contagem, in a border territory, exists the Confisco neighborhood, full of stories to tell.

But Moacir didn't give up because of that. It was then that he began to ask the class some questions: "So, guys, why do you think it's so bad to live here?", "Does anyone know the

---
[85] Freire, Paulo. (2011). *Pedagogia do oprimido*. Paz e Terra. p. 89.

neighborhood's history?", "Does anyone know why it has this name?".

Moacir invited the students to conduct a research project with him about the neighborhood's history and they agreed. One day, they all met at the school bleachers. The teacher brought a scale model of Confisco. It was beautiful, and the students got excited looking at the mini neighborhood in front of them. In a few moments, they began to recognize real locations inside the miniature. Some pointed to it in surprise when they found their homes.

Then, Moacir surprised them even more: he announced that, at that moment, two women who had founded the neighborhood were at the school. One of them was an employee, and the other was a community leader. Like a scavenger hunt, the kids were now to look for the answers about the neighborhood they didn't yet have. The difference is that, in the end, all would gain something – it wasn't a game that made a single person rich.

The students and the teacher now wanted to discover more and more – everything they could. Moacir and his interns went to the Minas Gerais' Public Archive (Arquivo Público Mineiro) and the Belo Horizonte's Public Archive (Arquivo Público de Belo Horizonte) to research the neighborhood's history. They collected old photos of Confisco and found news headlines, all negative. They took the results of their research to the class. That was when the "indignation class" happened – "the students were outraged by the headlines, it was a riot[86]".

Moacir opted to transform the class's anger into learning. Luiza, one of the interns, suggested that the class communicated the story they wanted to tell through photos. That was when she and other two interns offered a workshop

---

[86] Fragment of one of Teacher Moacir Fagundes' interviews for the field research.

teaching photography technique to the seventh-grade students. And then, the teaching reached the streets.

The kids went to the neighborhood's streets along with adults involved in the project. Besides taking photos, they interviewed residents to get to know more about their impression of Confisco, its living conditions, and if they had ever, for any reason, hidden that they lived there.

The researchers wanted to cover everything they didn't know about the neighborhood's history and would like to. Among the questions raised, the main ones were: "why the name 'Confisco'?; "from where had the residents come?; "why did they go to the neighborhood?"; and "what did the place look like when they got there?".

Questions about participatory budgeting were also asked since the researchers had already found out that the place known as "big hole" had been transformed through it. They wanted to get to know the neighborhood's history as told by its protagonists.

During this process, they noticed that Confisco's history was told by women, and discovered too that they were the quantitative majority of people in the squatting which originated the neighborhood. Most of these women were "single mothers" or divorced. In other cases, their partners worked far away from their homes – mainly in civil construction in the neighboring state of São Paulo. That was how the researchers discovered that, from the 38 houses nearest to the school, only three had men's names on their property deeds.

Amazed by this knowledge that wasn't contained in the history books, students and teacher started calling the neighborhood's original residents *"book-people"*. Since there weren't textbooks that talked about the community's origins, these women were that narrative's primary historical sources.

But they realized they could do even more – they could create their own books to write down the history they had heard about the Confisco's founders. That was how was the seventh-year class made Graça's dream come true and created the comic book about Confisco's history!

The comic book took to the streets and left the outskirts of the city: it got to Belo Horizonte's downtown and was projected on the Praça da Liberdade's buildings – a very important public space of the city. That was how the students put into practice what they wanted in the "indignation class". They made their own textbooks; they wrote the neighborhood's history and they were happy in the moment!

Now that you already know the general context of this history, I'll tell you some details. This time, through the voice of those who were interviewed. Before I do that, I present to you a thing Moacir said[87] when the comic books were being made:

> Anne said: "I want to write, but more than that, I want to bring out all kinds of things that lie buried deep in my heart.", and our students will say: "we want to bring out all kinds of things that lie in our neighborhood.".

In an interview for my field research, the teacher remembers:

> At the end of each interview, we gave each of them [the neighborhood's founders] a flowerpot. It was like we had put out a red carpet for them. They arrived at the school very happy, very empowered. **Their satisfaction in narrating their stories was evident. And the kids were there, attentive, recording it all, writing it all down. Within this process, the**

---

[87] Escola Municipal Anne Frank. (2016). *História do Confisco em Quadrinho*s.

book-person thing came up. **In the beginning, the kids started to ask: 'where will we research about the neighborhood?'.** I already knew that there was a collection within the Public Archive about the city's neighborhoods and that there was some information in newspapers, on the internet too – but little. **I showed them that there wasn't anything about the neighborhood in the library or the history textbook. 'It's history, isn't it? And why isn't the neighborhood's history within them?' – I asked that too.** [...] 'If the textbook doesn't say anything, how will we learn it?' 'Ah, let's interview the neighborhood's oldest residents!' **I started throwing hints that these people were knowledge sources and then a girl, Rayane, said: 'ah, teacher, I got it, they are people, and they are books too – because when we want to know something we look it up in books.** And then we started using this concept, I'm really proud that we came up with it. [...] I transcribed the interviews during the dawns – that was the teacher's job. **I spent many nights transcribing so that we could select the main themes that were talked about**

> in the interviews – not only the ones we had proposed but also those outside the themes we had initially brought up in them. [...] Within each theme, we selected something each *book-person* had said. We gave each quote a color and built a panel with them on the school's patio. *[emphasis added]*

At the end of this process, they tried to draw with the students a connection between the community's and Anne Frank's – the Holocaust victim that gave the school its name – histories. According to Moacir, just like the Jewish girl, the kids and teens from Confisco lived in the margins of the State and dwelled in an oppressive situation because of the place they occupied – because they lived in a marginalized neighborhood, and most of them were black and poor.

The school was helped by volunteers from the Universidade Federal de Minas Gerais (Federal University of Minas Gerais), the school's teachers, and people with direct and indirect relationships to the neighborhood that offered comic book, illustration and writing workshops to the students. During this period, field activities were conducted to photograph the neighborhood's residents and their daily lives. The students took about 600 to 700 photos, which were then printed and analyzed by the group, who chose 50 of them.

Moacir narrates:

> I really wanted everyone to participate, but when the activities happened outside of class time, I let them choose if they wanted to. I didn't pick the students who were to participate. My idea was that everyone would draw everything. I didn't want to choose, as if only the best ones would make the comic books. That wasn't my thinking. [...] The situation itself presented the solution. They all drew at some point, in one way or another. They drew the interviews, and the scenarios. Everybody did so. But when it came down to drawing the comic itself, together with the art teacher,

> Luciana – to transform the plot into drawing – several kids who had participated in the beginning left the task to others. 'Teacher, I can't do this character design thing. I tried, but João can do it, Kemily can.' They did this until the end, till there were three students: Ryan [Lucas], João Vítor [Souza], and Kemily [Pereira], who made the final drawings for the comic book. The dialogues, the theme, and the plot were created by everybody too. [...] Anne Frank joined as a special guest. The plot was: that she arrived in the neighborhood, which she did not know, and people came and introduced the territory to her. [...] One of them came up with the idea of making a time machine. There was a bug in the time machine and Anne Frank ended up in 2016 Confisco.

In the comic book, the history of the neighborhood is told by Anne Frank, who, in the narrative, goes to Confisco to learn about the community's history. The story was divided into seven parts: "Anne Frank in The Story of Confisco"; "Why 'Confisco'?"; "The Squatting"; "Two cities";

"Big Hole.... s... square!!"; "Anne Frank Municipal School"; and "Women's History".

At the comic book's release event, the students signed autographs in the school's auditorium for people from the community and family members. In addition, a photographic exhibition called "Confisco pelo Confisco" (Confisco by/for Confisco) was produced with photos taken by the students themselves, from their perspective, using equipment borrowed from the Universidade Federal de Minas Gerais (UFMG). With this, they intended to oppose the pejorative idea that the mainstream media built and spread about the neighborhood.

The exhibition was selected as an art show for UFMG's Espaço do Conhecimento (Knowledge Space) and stayed for about a month in one of Belo Horizonte's main localities: the Praça da Liberdade's Cultural Circuit. The 50 selected photos were projected on the wall of one of the cultural spaces that surround the Praça.

On the exhibition's opening night, the students were taken there. Moacir remembers:

> You should have seen their joy! Their happiness when they saw their names projected on the building's digital facade, the pictures they took. 'Look at my house, Carla's house. [...] There was applause, there was a choir. They started screaming, 'Ah, Anne Frank!'. [...] They were a big hit. The exhibition has already gone some other places: it was shown in the neighborhood square, at the Social Assistance Reference Center, at school, at the University, at the Pampulha Regional, you know? [...] It was a very collective, shared process. Another way of communicating. A better image of the neighborhood. [...] We have presented the project in conferences, colleges, museums [...] and we have given workshops on this methodology to teachers... on oral history and local history, on heritage [...] the project generated a lot of actions

> and opened a lot of possibilities. And to this day it hasn't stopped. [...] We won a national human rights award from the Ministry of Education and Culture, and, because of it, I represented the country in Cartagena, Colombia, in an educational seminar. So, the project has fulfilled its objective of spreading a positive image and narrative of the neighborhood, in contrast with the negative ones built by the media.

The exhibition "Confisco pelo Confisco" intended to create its own values, share its perspectives. It was, therefore, a means of disseminating what Augusto Boal called *the Aesthetics of the Oppressed*.

> It is not enough to consume culture: it is necessary to produce it. It is not enough to enjoy art: it is necessary to make art! It is not enough to think of ideas: it is necessary to transform them into social, concrete, and continuous acts.
> [...] **To be human is to be an artist!**

> **Art and Aesthetics are instruments of liberation**[88].
> *[emphasis from the original]*
> *[free translation]*

Still according to the author:

> Art is the object, material or immaterial. Aesthetics is the way to produce and perceive it. Art is inside the thing, Aesthetics, inside the subject and their gaze. There is knowledge that only the Symbolic Thought can give us; others, only the Senses are capable of illuminating. We cannot do without either of them.
>
> In the confrontation against the single thought, we have to be clear that politics is not the "art of doing what is possible", as is often said, but **the art of making possible what needs to be done. A citizen is not someone who lives in society – it's someone who transforms it!**
>
> **Art is not adornment, words are not absolute, sound is not noise, and images speak, convince and dominate. These three Powers –**

---

[88] Boal, Augusto. (2009). *A estética do oprimido*. Garamond. p. 19.

> **Word, Sound, and Image** – we cannot renounce, under the penalty of renouncing our **human condition**[89]. *[emphasis from the original] [free translation]*

By understanding themselves as creators of images and narratives of their territory, students and teacher mobilized two of the three powers that Augusto Boal recognizes as essential to the human condition.

Sandra Mara points out that this work led to the empowerment of community leaders, who came to see their narratives being valued, recognized, and disseminated by the school's community and, in a second moment, by the media. As Moacir tells:

> When we went to Brasília to receive the human rights in education award, they paid the

---

[89] Boal, Augusto. (2009). *A estética do oprimido*. Garamond. p. 22.

> travel expenses for me and Sandra, who was the School's Principal then. But we crowdfunded Graça's expenses too since she is one of the most active people in the community. [...] You should have seen how Graça was treated there, it was wonderful. She was the protagonist, and we were the supporting characters. It was like we had put out a red carped for her. After all, she was a living character from the story that was being told. She was both narrator and character. Everything she said carried a special legitimacy. What she has to say has a much greater value and weight than the Principal's narrative or mine. [...] She was revered. That, for me, was of immense value!

In addition, the former Principal narrated that the project transformed the lives of the teenagers involved. According to her,

> the girls and boys could now see that the neighborhood they lived in had a history and that the people telling it to them were proud of the struggle, the

victories, of everything they had built there. And the community's pride, these leaders' pride, in a way, reverberated in the boys and girls. So much so that I was able to follow some interviews for magazines with the kids and, in some of them – where people asked the children what they thought of the project – they said that they had learned to like their community through the stories told by these leaders. The stories of the first people who went there to build their homes, build their lives. And so, the media, which until then had a negative view of the community, started to have a positive one through the work of those students.

Within the comic book, Confisco's history is told from the strength and resilience of its community. The women who led the movement for decent housing in the territory had their stories and voices legitimized, the students were researchers and authors of their own history.

More than seeing themselves in the neighborhood, the comic book showed that they can be authors and characters of books. It showed them that their history too is legitimate and, therefore, that it has value. The comic book not only told alternative narratives, but it was also itself the materialization of a desired narrative.

The teacher highlights:

> There were several signals that the project was fulfilling its function. The first one was: if before it they said they didn't like the neighborhood, how come in the middle of the process they got outraged by newspapers headlines? [...] the second one was when **Ana Clara, who was one of the kids that denied the territory the most, said to a *book-person*:** 'How **come you went through so much to build the houses and people speak so badly of the neighborhood to this day? Wow, just like me, isn't it? I used to speak badly of it... but now I don't anymore, I only did so when I didn't know better.** [...] **And many people look for us wanting to add something to the story.** [...] **a battle of narratives has emerged.** This,

> for the historian, is very interesting. **There are a lot of people wanting to tell their version. The version told in the comic book isn't the only version of it. There's space for other versions and more research.** [...] I'm very proud of this project. [...] there are several different research paths that open up to continue the project: gender, local x world history, oral history, and the wonderful participation of two of our boys with disabilities. *[emphasis added]*

The project's success did not stop the teacher. On the contrary, he remains motivated and full of new dreams to fulfill in the community. As Moacir reminds us, "learning is incessant".

This is only the beginning. But, as we know, non-violent action demands starting stories from their beginning. Not without reason, RJ emerged first as practice, and only later as a theory.

I hope I have managed to narrate some of the fundamentals of Restorative Justice through respecting and honoring "what happened first". It was with this in mind that I set out to write this book. It was also for this purpose that I structured its three content chapters in the following order: Connection, Conflict, Violence.

May we, in our restorative trajectory, not forget that conflict and violence might demand urgent responses, but that the central point that structures restorative practice is connection. May we be aware that talking about RJ also demands attention to the danger of the single story.

Restorative action is not so much about what you do, but how you do it, including how you tell this story.

REFERENCES

Adichie, Chimamanda Ngozi. (2009, October 7th). *The danger of the single story.* YouTube. https://www.youtube.com/watch?v=D9Ihs241zeg.

Amaral Filho, Nemézio C. (2008). As perigosas fronteiras da "comunidade": um desafio à comunicação comunitária. In.: Paiva, Raquel; Santos, Cristiano Henrique Ribeiro dos. (Eds.). *Comunidade e contra-hegemonia: rotas de comunicação alternativa.* . Mauad X: FAPERJ.

Anderson, Benedict. (1993). *Comunidades imaginadas: reflexiones sobre el origen y la difusión del nacionalismo.* Cultura Libre.

Ashoka Brasil; Alana. *Escolas transformadoras: Sobre.* Escolas Transformadoras. http://escolastransformadoras.com.br/o-programa/sobre/.

Bhabha, Homi K. (2003). *O local da cultura*. Editora UFMG.

Boal, Augusto. (2009). *A estética do oprimido*. Garamond.

Bourdieu, Pierre. (2012). *O poder simbólico*. Bertrand Brasil.

Braithwaite, John. (2002). Does restorative justice work?. In: *Restorative justice and responsive regulation*. (pp. 45-72). Oxford University Press.

_____. (2006). Doing Justice Intelligently in Civil Society. *Journal of Social Issues*, 62(2). pp. 393-409.

BUBER, Martin. (2012). *Sobre comunidade*. Perspectiva

Carrillo, Alfonso Torres. (2017). *El retorno a la comunidad: problemas, debates y desafíos de vivir juntos.* Fundación Centro Internacional de Educación y Desarrollo Humano

Calvo Soler, Raúl. (2014). *Mapeo de conflictos: técnica para la exploración de los conflictos.* Gedisa.

Carvalho, Mayara. (2019). *Justiça Restaurativa na Comunidade: uma experiência em Contagem-MG.*

Carvalho, Mayara; Coelho, Juliana. (2018). Autocomposição judicial: o meio mais rápido e barato para a macdonaldização das decisões? Análise segundo o CPC que ama muito tudo isso. In.: Cordeiro, Juliana; Norato, Ester; Marx Neto, Edgard. *Novas tendências: diálogos entre direito material e processual.* D'Plácido.

Carvalho, Mayara; Jeronimo, Lucas; Silva, Elaine Cristina da. (2020). *Comunicação Não-Violenta: diálogos e reflexões.* Instituto Pazes.

Center for Justice and Peacebuilding. (2017). Strategies for Trauma Awareness and Resilience: Level I Participant Manual. Eastern Mennonite University.

Centro de Referência Popular do Bairro do Confisco. (2014, March 21). *Histórico do Conjunto Confisco.* Facebook. https://www.facebook.com/confiscobh/posts/hist%C3%B3rico-do-conjunto-confiscoo-conjunto-confisco-nasceu-em-1988-e-est%C3%A1-localiza/440726819404942/.

Coutinho, Eduardo (Director). (1987). *Santa Marta: duas semanas no morro.* [Documentary] Ministério da Justiça.

Deutsch, Morton. (2004). A resolução do conflito. In: Azevedo, Andre Gomma de. (Ed.). *Estudos em arbitragem, negociação e mediação.* (pp. 29-44). UNB.

_____. Cooperation, Conflict, and Justice. In.: BIERHOFF Deutsch, Morton. (1986). Cooperation, Conflict, and Justice. In.: Bierhoff, Hans Wermer; Cohen, Ronald; Greenberg, Jerald. (Eds.). *Justice in Social Relations.* Ontario: Melvin J. Lerner, 1986.

_____. Deutsch, Morton. (2014). Cooperation, Competition, and Conflict. In.: Coleman, Peter; Deutsch, Morton; Marcus, Eric. (Eds.). *The handbook of conflict resolution: theory and practice*. Jossey-Bass

Ephesus, Heraclitus of. (2013). *Heráclito: los fragmentos*. Laodamia Press.

Escola Municipal Anne Frank. (2016). *História do Confisco em Quadrinhos*.

Estés, Clarissa Pinkola. (2017). *Women who run with the Wolves: myths and stories of the wild woman archetype.* River Wolf Press.

Fanon, Frantz. (1967). *Black Skin, White Masks*. Grove Press.

Freire, Paulo. (2011). *Pedagogia do oprimido*. Paz e
Terra.

Gade, Christian B. N. (2018). "Restorative Justice": History of the Term's International and Danish Use. In.: Nylund, Anna; Ervasti, Kaijus; Adrian, Lin. (Eds.). *Nordic Mediation Research*. Springer.

Halaby, Mona Hajja. (2000). *Belonging: creating community in the classroom*. Brookline Books.

Holman, Peggy. (2010). *Engaging emergence: turning upheaval into opportunity*. Berret Koehler.

_____. (1999). *The change handbook: group methods for shaping the future*. Berret Koehler.

Jupiara, Aloy; Otavio, Chico. (2015). *Os porões da contravenção: jogo do bicho e ditadura militar: a história da aliança que profissionalizou o crime organizado*. Record.

Kiva International. *Evidence of effectiveness in Finland and elsewhere*. Kiva Program. https://www.kivaprogram.net/kiva-is-effective/.

Lederach, John Paul. (2005). *The moral imagination: the art and soul of building peace*. Oxford University Press

_____. (2012). *Transformação de conflitos*. Palas Athena.

Leminski, Paulo. (2013). *Toda Poesia*. Companhia das Letras.

Levinas, Emmanuel. (1991). *Ética e infinito*. La balsa de la Medusa.

_____. (2014). *Violência do rosto*. Loyola.

Machado, Regina. (2015). *A arte da palavra e da escuta.* Reviravolta.

Mackay, Robert E. (2013). The nexus between rights and restorative justice: using a case example of an organization 'C' – the right – or moral and spiritual claim – to recognition. In.: Gravielides, Theo; Artinopoulou, Vasso. *Reconstructing restorative justice philosophy*. Ashgate Publishing Limited.

Melo, M.B.P. (2013). (Re)pensar a violência escolar à luz das estratégias de intervenção em territórios de intervenção prioritária. In: Maria Manuel Vieira, José Resende, Maria Alice Nogueira, Juarez Dayrell, Alexandre Martins, António Calha (Eds.). *Habitar a escola e as suas margens: geografias plurais em confronto.* (pp. 157-169). Portalegre: Escola Superior de Educação, Instituto Politécnico de Portalegre.

Nader, Laura, (1994). Harmonia coercitiva: a economia política dos modelos jurídicos. *Revista Brasileira de Ciências Sociais,* 9 (26). https://anpocs.com/images/stories/RBCS/26/rbcs26_02.pdf.

Olb Jon; Parry, Madeleine. (2018). *Hannah Gadsby: Nanette* [Live Comedy Performance]. Netflix.

Parker, Christine. (1999). Public Rights in Private Government: Corporate Compliance with Sexual Harassment Legislation. *Australian Journal of Human Rights,* 6, 5(1), p. 159-193.

http://classic.austlii.edu.au/au/journals/AUJlHRights/1999/6.html

Peck, Raoul (Director). (2016). *I am not your Negro* [Film]. Velvet Film; Artemis Productions; Close Up Films.

Pranis, Kay. (2010). *Processos circulares*. Palas Athenas; Pranis, Kay

Pranis, Kay; Stuart, Barry; Wedge, Mark. (2003) Circles: a paradigm shift in how we respond to crime. In.: _____. *Peacemaking circles: from conflict to community*. Living Justice Press.

Rede Minas. Jornal Minas. (2018). *Série Confisco: História Revista – Episódio 1*. Youtube. https://www.youtube.com/watch?v=wM86YIgFe-A

_____. (2018). *Série Confisco: História Revista – Episódio 2*. YouTube. https://www.youtube.com/watch?v=75z_K7DtFAI&feature=youtu.be.

_____. (2018). *Série Confisco: História Revista – Episódio 3*. YouTube. https://www.youtube.com/watch?v=73fTyKoB5X.

Ricoeur, Paul. (2008). *Outramente: leitura do livro Autrement qu'être ou au- delà de l'essence de Emmanuel Lévinas*. Vozes.

Sabetti, Stèphano. (2015). *The path of no way: a spiritual primer: introduction to essential inquiry and process mediation*. Boston: Life energy media.; Tolle, Eckhart. (2010). O poder do agora. Sextante.

Sahlins, Marshall. (2013). *Heráclito x Heródoto*. In: _____ Esperando Foucault, ainda. Cosac Naif, 2013. p. 16.

Sartre, Jean-Paul. (1985). *Réflexions sur la question juive.* Paris Gallimard.

Schwarcz, Lilia Moritz; Starling, Heloisa Murgel. (2015). *Brasil: uma biografia*. Companhia das Letras.

Segato, Rita Laura. (2006). *Antropologia e direitos humanos: alteridade e ética no movimento de expansão dos direitos universais.* MANA, 12(1). pp.207- 236.

_____. (2003). La argamassa jerárquica: violencia moral, reproducción del mundo y la eficácia simbólica del Derecho. In.: _____. *Las estructuras elementales de la violencia: ensayos sobre género entre la antropologia, el psicoanálisis y los derechos humano*s. Universidad Nacional de Quilmes.

Senge, Peter; et al. (2005). *Presence: exploring profound change in people, organizations, and society.* Nicholas Brealey Publishing

Sherman, Lawrence; Strang, Heather. (2007). *Restorative Justice: the evidence.* The Smith Institute.

Spivak, Gayatri Chakravorty. (2014). Pode o subalterno falar?. Editora UFMG.

Tolle, Eckhart. (2010). *O poder do agora*. Sextante.

Travisan, Maria Carolina. *O Brasil é o país que mais mata por arma de fogo no mundo*. Flacso Brasil. http://flacso.org.br/?publication=o-brasil-e-o-pais-que-mais-mata-por-arma-de-fogo-no-mundo.

United Nations Development Programme. (2007). *Democratic Dialogue: a handbook for practitioners*. International Idea.

Yoder, Carolyn E.; Barge, Elaine Zook. (2012). *Strategies for Trauma Awareness and Resilience: The Unfolding Story*. Center for Justice and Peacebuilding.

Zehr, Howard. (2015). *Changing lenses: restorative justice for our times*. (Twenty-fifth-anniversary edition). Herald Press.

Zellerer, Evelyn. (2013). *Realizing the potential of restorative justice*. In.: Gravielides, Theo; Artinopoulou, Vasso. *Reconstructing restorative justice philosophy*. Ashgate Publishing Limited.

ABOUT THE AUTHOR: ACADEMIC PATH

Mayara Carvalho is one of co-founders of the Instituto Pazes. She has earned her Ph.D. in Law from the Universidade Federal de Minas Gerais (Brazil), with research in Community Restorative Justice. She's done her masters in Legal Sciences at the Universidade Federal da Paraíba (Brazil) and got her Bachelor's from the Universidade Federal do Rio Grande do Norte. She is also a postdoctoral researcher in Restorative Justice at the Universidade Estadual do Rio de Janeiro's Postgraduate Program in Law (Brazil).

She's a teacher and former coordinator of the PUC Minas Restorative Justice specialization, and a teacher at the Universidade Estácio de Sá's Postgraduate Program. She is a teacher, researcher, and facilitator of restorative and nonviolent communication practices.

She also is an evaluator in several legal and human sciences journals. She was a content teacher at the Programa NÓS de Justiça Restaurativa (Centers for Guidance and Resolution of School Conflicts Restorative Justice Program), having helped in the design and implementation of the program in state and municipal schools in Belo Horizonte.

She was an Ecumenical Accompanier in Palestine and Israel (EAPPI/WCC), where she monitored human rights violations, offered a protective presence to vulnerable groups, and provided humanitarian assistance. Lastly, she's also a member of the Comissão de Justiça Restaurativa do Fórum Socioeducativo de Belo Horizonte (Restorative Justice Commission of the Socio-educational Forum of Belo Horizonte).

Publications:

https://mayaracarvalho.academia.edu/research

Contact info:

mdecarvalho@live.com

www.pazes.com.br

Instagram: @maylizarb

Instagram: @institutopazes

ABOUT THE AUTHOR: MY WORDS

I was born in Natal, by the sea. Does a beautiful, but full of violence city sound familiar to you? This mixture of beauty and amazement disturbed me deeply. I was so afraid of all that hate and violence that, from an early age, I started to study and get involved with these themes.

When I got into college, I still wasn't sure where to go, but I was aware of what had led me there: I wanted to work with conflict and violence prevention.

So, I went on... working with Restorative Justice, human rights, and conflict transformation. And that was when two experiences substantially changed the direction I had been following in my life:

My time working with humanitarian aid and with war conflicts in Palestine and Israel touched me deeply. I was no longer the same person – I had seen and learned about a new world and other ways of building relationships and peace.

The second experience was my Ph.D. research. I had been studying community-based restorative justice and was already on my way to present my thesis when I asked myself: "who do I think I am to say I'm 'doctor of community justice' if I haven't truly sought this common-in-me yet?".

I slowed down and tried to get in touch with my narratives and experiences of support. I found coherence first. When the Ph.D. degree arrived, it wasn't even that important anymore, but it rang true to me. I keep discovering the common-in-me, but now it makes even more sense to see myself one-with-everything-that-is.

ABOUT THE TRANSLATOR

Júlia Muinhos is a Restorative Justice (RJ) facilitator, researcher, and translator (Portuguese to English and vice versa). As a law student at the Universidade Federal de Minas Gerais, Júlia has experience coordinating courses, cases, and supervision activities. Júlia's current RJ research focuses on the Transitional Restorative Justice processes occurring in Greensboro, North Carolina.

Beyond the RJ arena, Júlia works with International Human Rights (currently as an intern under Henrique Napoleão Alves' Office) and Human Rights research under the Universidade Federal de Minas Gerais' Human Rights Clinic.

Contact info:
E-mail: ju.muinhos@gmail.com

Linkedin: www.linkedin.com/in/júlia-muinhos-8a0840217

We thank you for making it this far!

Instituto Pazes
Belo Horizonte, 2022

www.ingramcontent.com/pod-product-compliance
Lightning Source LLC
Chambersburg PA
CBHW031624210526
45464CB00004B/1737